THE WOMEN'S SUFFRAGE COOKERY BOOK

Compiled by
MRS. AUBREY DOWSON

Foreword by
POLLY RUSSELL
Curator for Contemporary Politics and
Public Life at the British Library

Foreword

At first glance, the recipes inside *The Women's Suffrage Cookery Book* for cream cheese sandwiches or apple and sago pudding do not seem to invite rebellion, resistance or revolution but this is exactly what they were intended to do. Compiled by Mrs Aubrey Dowson, a member of the Birmingham branch of the National Union of Women Suffrage Societies (NUWSS), this unassuming cookery book was published in 1912 by the Women's Printing Society Limited to raise funds for a radical cause – votes for women.

The Women's Printing Society was set up in the 1870s by the suffragists Emily Faithfull and Emma Paterson. Way ahead of its time, it was run as a cooperative and trained women in the printing trade, a field traditionally restricted to men.

The book contains recipes donated by suffragists from all across the country, including some well-known campaigners. Millicent Fawcett, founder of the NUWSS suggests a recipe for Chestnuts as a Vegetable (page 33) and Mrs Helena Swanwick, the one-time editor of the suffrage newspaper *Common Cause,* offers one for Stuffed Filleted Plaice (page 21). With contributors from as far afield as Southport and Penrith, the book is evidence of the campaign's national reach.

For suffragists, a cookery book was a practical way to deploy their 'womanly' skills and knowledge. It was also an implicit rebuttal to the idea that suffragists were neglectful mothers, failed wives and home-breakers. *The Women's Suffrage Cookery Book* is a reminder that suffragists were not looking to overturn women's relation to the home but to increase their agency within it.

By 1903, with no sign of the government relenting and granting women the vote, Emmeline Pankhurst set up the Women's Social and Political Union, a militant organization, whose motto was 'Deeds not Words'. The violent actions of the suffragettes – the term coined by the *Daily Express* to describe the militants – are perhaps better remembered than the tireless but ultimately less dramatic antics of the law-abiding NUWSS members. Debate reigns as to whether the lawbreakers or the lawful were more instrumental in winning the vote for women, but despite strategic differences, tenacity, ingenuity and courage were common to both. *The Women's Suffrage Cookery Book* suggests that humour and wit played a part, too: at the end of the book the wife of philosopher and political activist Bertrand Russell, Alys Pearsall Smith, pens a five-step recipe 'For Cooking and Preserving a Good Suffrage Speaker'. The first instruction is to 'Butter the speaker' and the fourth to 'Beat her to a froth with an optimistic spoon'.

In the end it took more than 50 years of hard campaigning, the combined efforts of militant suffragettes and law-abiding suffragists and a World War to swing public opinion and persuade the government to allow women the vote. I like to think that, as well as the petitions, protests, prison sentences and hunger strikes, baked bananas, egg croquettes and the meals and menus proposed by *The Women's Suffrage Cookery Book* also played a part.

Polly Russell, 2020

Dr Polly Russell is Lead Curator for Contemporary Politics and Public Life at the British Library. She is also a food historian and co-presenter of the BBC's *Back in Time for . . .* series. Polly has been the British Library lead in a number of research collaborations including the Leverhulme-funded 2012–2015 'Sisterhood & After: The Women's Liberation Movement Oral History Project' with the University of Sussex. She also led the project to digitise the entire run of *Spare Rib* magazines in order to make them freely available on the internet.

Publisher's Note

This book is a faithful facsimile of a book published in 1912. A few terms, ingredients, and equipment have since fallen out of common usage and may need to be substituted with modern equivalents. To preserve the authenticity of the original publication no terms have been changed, and the recipes have not been tested or altered in any way. The publisher cannot take any responsibility for damages or losses resulting from the instructions herein. The reader should seek medical advice if they suffer from allergies and wear protective gloves for recipes which include materials that may be irritants in the Miscellanies chapter.

See the Glossary on page 78 for explanations of unfamiliar terms.
See also Useful Weights and Measures on page 63.

CONTENTS.

Breakfast Dishes

Egg Croquettes

5 eggs boiled hard	Pepper
1 oz. of butter	Teaspoonful of chopped parsley
1 oz. of flour	A little onion
Salt	1 raw egg

Make the mixture into sausage-shape rolls, egg and breadcrumb them. Fry in boiling fat.

Mrs. JULIAN OSLER, Edgbaston.

Egg Patties

Boil 6 eggs hard, chop fine, and mix 2 tablespoonfuls of breadcrumbs, a tomato cut small, a little thyme, pepper and salt. Line some patty pans with paste, put in the mixture, cover, and bake in a rather hot oven. Serve either hot or cold.

Miss SHEPPARD, London.

French Eggs

Boil the eggs for half an hour, allow 1 egg for each person, then take whites and chop up finely, leaving yolks to be used last. To each egg allow 1 oz. of butter, 1 teaspoonful of flour, 2 teaspoonfuls of milk, pepper and salt to taste. Put into a saucepan and boil up; spread on hot buttered toast and grate the yolks over the top.

Mrs. J. K. REID, Edgbaston.

Galettes de Pommes de Terre

Bake or boil 12 nice floury potatoes and peel them, pass through a fine colander, mix with them 2 ozs. of butter, 4 eggs, a little salt and chopped-up parsley. Take a spoonful of the mixture, shake it in a floured tumbler until it is a ball, then put it on to your pasteboard and flatten out with roller to half-an-inch thickness, cut round (with edge of the tumbler). Take a very clean frying-pan, make some butter very hot in it and put in the galettes, fry a nice brown and serve very hot.

Miss SHEPPARD, London.

Œufs sur le plat

Melt some butter in a French earthenware fireproof dish. Then break into the butter carefully enough eggs to cover the dish, add pepper and salt and bake in a moderate oven for a few minutes until the eggs are lightly set. This is a delicious breakfast dish. The melted butter should just cover the bottom of the dish, which must of course come to table as it is. The proper dishes are sold everywhere where fireproof china is sold. They must have covers and are not at all unsightly. Mrs. MORGAN WILLIAMS, Swansea.

Omelette

Break 6 eggs into a basin, with salt, pepper and finely chopped herbs (spring onions also, chopped fine, if liked). Add 1 spoonful of water and beat it 4 minutes, and then put in a piece of butter (size of a large filbert nut). Melt 2 ozs. of butter in the frying-pan, then pour in the mixture and with a knife separate the part that sets from the frying-pan, and let the liquid part go underneath (it must never stick). When not quite set slide it into the hot dish and double it over, and serve at once. Miss SHEPPARD, London.

Dried Haddock and Tomatoes

1 dried haddock	1 oz. of butter
1 small onion	Pepper and salt
2 tomatoes	Parsley

Soak the fish for 10 minutes, then skin it, take out all the bones and break up the fish into flakes, slice the onion and tomatoes, chop up the parsley, sprinkle with pepper and salt and cook all in the butter till quite soft, then add the fish and cook for 10 minutes longer. Dish up in a border of boiled rice or mashed potato. Mrs. WALTER COHEN, Berkhamsted.

Lobster Omelette

2 eggs	2 tablespoonfuls of good white sauce
2 tablespoonfuls of cream	flavoured with anchovy
or milk	Salt and pepper to taste
1 oz. of butter	

Beat up the eggs, whites and yolks separately, mix the cream with the yolks, then both together with salt and pepper. Have a clear fire and put the butter into the omelette pan, and when it begins to bubble pour in the mixture and keep stirring until it thickens, but care must be taken not to cook it too much. When it is nicely browned on the bottom, spread on the lobster, which should be previously cut into small pieces and made hot in the sauce, fold in half and serve at once.

This is sufficient for two persons. Miss NORA G. PARR, Lapworth.

Salmon Croquettes

1 tin of salmon, or	A few drops of carmine (if liked)
1 lb. of fresh salmon	6 ozs. of butter
1 flat teaspoonful of mustard	2 lbs. of potatoes
½ teaspoonful of white pepper	1 tablespoonful of vinegar
¼ teaspoonful of cayenne	1 teaspoonful of French mustard (if liked)

Drain juice from salmon, remove skin and bones or any dark pieces, flavour with mustard, pepper, cayenne and carmine and pound in a mortar. Then add the potato mashed, the vinegar and French mustard. Flour hands and make the mixture into balls and fry.

Miss FLORENCE M. BUCKLEY, Crawley Down.

Baked Bananas

Take some not too ripe bananas and lay on the bar of an ordinary fire and leave until the skins are quite black. To be eaten very hot. They can of course be baked in an oven but the result is less satisfactory. The bananas should not be peeled, but should be lightly slit with a fork down one side, and the contents eaten with a spoon.

Miss ATHYA, Southport.

Beef Roll

1 lb. of beef	2 eggs
½ lb. of bacon or ham	Seasoning
¼ lb. of breadcrumbs	

Pass the meat through a mincing machine, mix it well with breadcrumbs, seasoning and egg, tie it in a cloth very tight, like a roly-poly, boil for 3 hours, take it out of the cloth and put grated crumbs over it. Serve cold for lunch or breakfast.

Mrs. JULIAN OSLER, Edgbaston.

Breakfast Roll

3 lbs. of chicken, lamb, or veal	¼ lb. of ham or tongue
¼ lb. of breadcrumbs	Season with herbs, pepper, salt and cayenne

Beat 3 eggs and mix with above, tie up in a cloth like a roly-poly and boil for 2½ hours. When cold glaze.

Mrs. GAYTON, Merstham.

Kidney Toast

Chop up very fine some mutton kidney, season with salt, pepper and a little cayenne. Toss it over the fire in a stewpan with a little butter until cooked, but not overdone. Have ready some slices of hot buttered toast, and just before putting on the toast, add to the kidneys, off the fire, the beaten-up yolk of an egg and a squeeze or two of lemon. Spread the mixture on the toast, put it in the oven to get quite hot, and serve immediately.

Mrs. H. P. Cobb, Harrow Weald.

Potahoi

An Indian breakfast dish for one person

A piece of butter the size of a walnut, a large (or 2 small ones) tomato cut in pieces and cooked till tender in the butter, with (if liked) a teaspoonful of minced onion and half a red pepper minced, or pepper, and very little salt. Add an egg well beaten, stir all together and cook till a nice consistency and serve.

Mrs. Brackenbury, Gomshall.

Luncheon Dishes

———— ✦ ————

FISH AND MEAT, ETC:

Beef Cutlets

Cut the under part of a sirloin of beef into nice slices, egg and breadcrumb them. Have ready a good gravy thickened, put in the slices and let them simmer, not boil, from a quarter to half an hour.

Mrs. H. P. Cobb, Harrow Weald.

Beef or Mutton stewed in its own gravy

A piece of rump steak, a chump chop, or a thick slice from the middle of a leg of mutton may be used. Trim away the fat and skin, just dip into cold water, let it drain an instant, then sprinkle on both sides with pepper, and flour rather thickly. Lay the meat flat in a stewpan which has been rinsed with cold water, of which a tablespoonful should be left in. Keep it just simmering over a *very* gentle fire for an hour and a half to three-quarters. Add salt when it begins to boil and turn when rather more than half done. Two spoonfuls of gravy, well seasoned, may be added if liked.

Miss Warren, Hampstead.

Cold Meat and Batter

Make a thick batter with:

½ lb. of flour	A pinch of salt
1 teaspoonful of baking powder	½ pint of milk

Cut the meat into neat pieces, immerse them in the batter, take them out again in spoonfuls, drop them into boiling fat and fry till brown.

Miss May Laurence, Penrith.

Curry

Take about 2 lbs. of the best end of neck of mutton or breast of veal. Cut it into pieces about the size of a lump of sugar. Take 2 medium sized onions, cut them into rings, fry them lightly brown with 2 ozs. of butter. Have ready 1 tablespoonful of Vencatechellum's curry powder and 1 dessertspoonful of curry paste; pour the liquid butter from the frying-pan on to it and make it into a paste. Add the fried onion and the meat to the curry mixture, also a teaspoonful of salt and a half pint of water or stock and threepenny-worth of cream. Stir them all together and let it simmer very gently for 2 hours.

Mrs. JULIAN OSLER, Edgbaston.

Egg Cutlets

3 eggs freshly boiled very hard, chop them very fine. Make a nice white sauce rather stiff, mix in the eggs, pepper and salt them and spread on a plate to cool, then shape the mixture into cutlets, egg and breadcrumb them and fry.

These make a good first dish for luncheon.

Miss MARY TANNER, London.

Fish Pudding

1 lb. of cold cooked fish	Salt and pepper
3 ozs. of breadcrumbs	1 gill (or more) of fish stock or milk
2 eggs	(Oysters if desired)

Mince fish, beat up eggs and mix all together. Butter basin and dust with breadcrumbs and either steam or bake for 1 hour. Serve with fish sauce, garnish with parsley and hard-boiled yolk of egg.

Mrs. BRACKENBURY, Gomshall.

Mixed Grill

Composed of

Sheep's tongues	Kidneys
Brains	Fried bread
Chicken livers	

Stew the tongues gently for 3 or 4 hours in stock (or Lemco). Stew the kidneys gently for 3 or 4 hours separately. *Hard boil* the brains in water, strain and let them get cold, then fry them (as you would cutlets). Fry the livers in butter, cut the bread in small rounds and fry golden brown in butter and place them on a hot dish with the different "items" upon them. The tongues should be halved, cut lengthwise. A tomato cut and fried may be added, the skin first removed by plunging in boiling water.

Mrs. ATKINSON, Camberley.

Patna Rice and Tomatoes

½ lb. of boiled Patna rice

1 lb. of tinned tomatoes

1 oz. or more of butter

Pepper and salt

Small quantity of chopped onion

Boil rice in water 20 minutes and strain. Put into a frying-pan some butter and melt, add rice, tomatoes and onion, and fry 10 minutes. Stir well and serve very *hot* in vegetable dish with steak or cutlets.

Mrs. BERNARD DAWSON, Geldeston.

Rabbit Cream

Cut away all the meat from a raw rabbit and put through the mincing machine, then pound in a mortar with an egg, salt and pepper, and a very little nutmeg, pound well and then pass through a very fine wire or hair sieve, mix with a gill of cream, put in mould and steam 20 minutes. Pour over a cream bechamel sauce.

Mrs. PELHAM LANE, King's Norton.

Risotta à la Milanaise

(For two persons)

2 ozs. of fresh butter

1 onion

½ lb. of East India rice

A very little powdered saffron

1 pint of stock or beef tea

A little grated nutmeg

A little grated Parmesan

Put 2 ozs. of fresh butter with an onion chopped very fine into a stewpan and fry until the onion has a pale gold colour, then add the rice, well washed, with a very little powdered saffron, stirring it constantly for about 2 minutes with a wooden spoon so that it does not stick to the saucepan; after this add the stock very gradually, let it simmer gently, stirring frequently till the rice is just soft. Before it is quite finished add the grated nutmeg and Parmesan.

Mrs. GAYTON, Merstham.

Roman Pudding

This may be made with any cooked meat. Take 1 lb. (more or less) of minced meat, ¼ lb. of breadcrumbs, a cupful of macaroni (soaked) mixed and well seasoned, moisten with a well-beaten egg and a little gravy and put the mixture into a well-buttered basin or mould. Boil for an hour and a half. Turn out into a hot dish and serve with some good brown gravy round the pudding. It looks better if the basin has been lined with macaroni before the mixture is put in.

Miss LOWRY, Chester.

Salisbury Roll

¾ lb. of lean beef steak	1 egg
¼ lb. of ham	A little nutmeg
2 ozs. of breadcrumbs	Pepper and salt to taste

Mince the meat up finely, add the breadcrumbs, then the seasoning, and mix with egg. Form into roll, tie firmly with a cloth and boil gently for 3 hours. When the cloth is removed, scatter browned breadcrumbs thickly over roll, or glaze.

Miss JOYCE SEYMER THOMPSON, Cambridge.

"Scotch Eggs"

(Cold dish for supper or luncheon)

7 eggs
Sausages (about 2 lbs.)
Breadcrumbs

Hard boil 6 of the eggs; put the sausages into boiling water for 3 minutes, then take out and remove skins; shell the eggs and wrap in sausage meat (2 sausages to each egg), shape into a nice firm oval, roll in egg and breadcrumbs and fry in boiling fat. When cold, cut in half shortways and garnish with parsley and watercress.

Miss JANET HAMILTON THOMPSON, Highgate.

Tomato Pie

Peel and skin as many ripe tomatoes as will be required, put a layer of bread-crumbs at the bottom of a pie-dish, then a layer of tomatoes, upon which sprinkle pepper and salt, a little vinegar, and add small lumps of butter. Then put another layer of tomatoes with again pepper, salt and butter. Do this until the dish is full. Let a layer of breadcrumbs be at the top, upon which put enough butter to brown in the oven. Bake until the tomatoes are quite soft and the top nicely browned. The time depends a good deal upon the ripeness of the tomatoes and the heat of the oven.

Mrs. MORGAN WILLIAMS, Swansea.

Turkish Pilace

6 ozs. of East India rice	Salt
1 pint of water	Pepper
1 oz. of butter	½ pint of good fowl broth

Wash well the rice and boil in the water for 8 or 10 minutes at the most. Throw into a colander so that it may thoroughly drain, then place it in a stewpan with 1 oz. of butter, salt and pepper to taste; stirring well and adding by degrees about half a pint of fowl broth. In about 15 minutes or so it should be properly done, turning out with the grains separate. It is to be served very hot.

The foregoing is a true Pilace but additions may be made of portions of the meat of the fowl or other meat, of curry powder, chutney, or fried onions, mushrooms, etc.

Mrs. GAYTON, Merstham.

Veal Paté

3 lbs. of uncooked veal chopped very fine

¼ lb. of salt pork or bacon

1 cup of pounded cracker crumbs

3 eggs

½ cupful of butter

3 teaspoonfuls of salt

2 teaspoonfuls of black pepper

1 nutmeg

Knead until well mixed, bake in oven in deep pan for 2 hours. When cold cut into slices.

Mrs. E. M. GARDNER, Edgbaston.

PUDDINGS

Almswood Pudding

2 ozs. of butter

2 ozs. of sugar

½ pint of milk

2 ozs. of flour

2 eggs

A little flavouring

Beat the butter and sugar together, beat the eggs together and add them; next add flour and then milk, taking care that all are *well beaten*. Put the mixture into a pie-dish and bake for 40 minutes in a warm oven. Serve immediately on taking it out of the oven.

Miss JULIA SHARP, Great Missenden.

Apple Beggarman

Pare, slice and stew in a little water, 1½ lbs. of good cooking apples; when quite soft mash them up and mix with half the quantity of breadcrumbs, some sugar, the grated rind and a little juice of a lemon, some chopped sultanas or currants, a little finely chopped candied peel and the yolk of two eggs. Well butter a pie-dish, line it with breadcrumbs and put the mixture in. Bake till firm, then cover with a meringue of the whites of the eggs, and brown slightly. Serve hot or cold.

Mrs. GAYTON, Merstham.

Economical Lemon Cream

1 quart of milk	2 large lemons
8 bitter almonds	¾ lb. of loaf sugar
2 ozs. of gelatine	Yolks of 6 eggs

Put the milk into a lined saucepan with the almonds (well pounded in a mortar), the gelatine, lemon rind and loaf sugar, and boil for about 5 minutes. Beat up the yolks of the eggs, strain the milk into a jug, add the eggs and pour the mixture backwards and forwards until nearly cold; then stir briskly to it the lemon juice (strained) and keep stirring until the cream is nearly cold; put it into an oiled mould. The lemon juice must not be added to the cream when it is warm and it should be well stirred after it is put in.

Mrs. DOWSON, Gorleston-on-Sea.

Fairyland Pudding

Put 1 pint of cold water with 6 ozs. of loaf sugar and rind of 2 lemons. Let it boil until the sugar is dissolved; mix 2 ozs. of cornflour with the juice of 2 lemons and stir into boiling water, boil until thickened, then beat the whites of 2 eggs to a stiff froth and add to the mixture, and pour into a damp mould.

Mrs. BUCKLEY, Edgbaston.

Light Dumplings
(Much liked)

½ lb. of flour	1 teaspoonful of baking powder
½ teaspoonful of salt	

Mix into a smooth clean paste (very quickly) with cold water. Roll into dumplings and drop at once into *fast boiling* water in a fairly large saucepan. Put lid on tight and BOIL FAST for 20 minutes. Serve quickly on a hot dish with hot treacle in a sauce tureen handed to eat with it. On no account lift the lid during the boiling or the dumplings will be heavy.

Mrs. GAYTON, Merstham.

Llanberis Pudding

2 eggs	3 tablespoonfuls of raspberry jam
The same weight in flour and butter	1 teaspoonful of carbonate of soda
And half the weight in loaf sugar	

Melt the butter with the carbonate of soda, mix this with the other ingredients. Butter a mould, half fill it with the mixture, and steam for 2½ hours.

Sauce: Pare the rind of 2 lemons very fine, and cut it into narrow strips, steep in a large cup of water with the juice of 2 lemons and 6 lumps of sugar. Simmer all on the fire for 15 minutes and pour hot over the pudding directly it is turned out, leaving the lemon straws on the top.

Mrs. W. RYLAND, Edgbaston.

Orange Pudding

½ lb. of sugar in lumps well rubbed on the rind of 3 oranges (previously washed). Put this in a basin and squeeze the juice of the oranges over it. Let it stand for several hours until the sugar is quite dissolved. Break 5 eggs into another basin, beat them slightly until they are quite mixed, but not risen. Add the juice and sugar by stirring all the time. Butter a mould and steam 1 hour.

For Sauce: Take the juice of 1 orange and 1 lemon, add castor sugar by degrees to the whites of 3 eggs, beaten to a froth, and simmered a little in the steamer after the pudding is taken out, beating all the time.

Mrs. BRACKENBURY, Gomshall.

Plum Charlotte

6 ozs. of breadcrumbs	3 ozs. of brown sugar
3 ozs. of Hugon's suet or butter	4 or 5 plums

Mix well, butter a basin, put in a thick layer of the mixture; cut about 4 or 5 plums in halves (take out the stones), sprinkle sugar over them and cover with the rest of the mixture, press down, bake in a sharp oven and turn out when brown.

Miss G. E. SOUTHALL, Edgbaston.

Portuguese Fritters

¼ lb. of Carolina rice	4 lumps of sugar
2 ozs. of castor sugar	2 eggs (yolks only)
2 ozs. of butter	Lemon peel
1 pint of milk	

Wash the rice well and put it into a saucepan with the milk. Boil nearly an hour, stirring frequently to prevent the milk boiling over. When thoroughly soft draw to the side of the fire and add the yolks of 2 eggs, 4 lumps of sugar rubbed on a lemon and pounded up with 2 ozs. of castor sugar. Stir all well into the rice and then pour the mixture on to a plate to cool. When cold roll the rice paste into balls on a floured board, egg and breadcrumb and fry. Hot golden syrup makes a good sauce to serve with them.

Miss WARREN, Hampstead.

Railway Pudding

1 teacupful of flour	1 egg
1 teacupful of castor sugar	½ gill of milk
2 teaspoonfuls of baking powder	

Sieve flour and sugar into a basin, beat up egg and add milk in another basin; add baking powder to the flour and sugar, then pour in the milk. Put into a well-buttered Yorkshire pudding tin as quickly as possible and bake directly in a hot oven. When baked, take the pudding from the tin, cut it into pieces, and serve with jam or plain with fruit.

Mrs. P. W. CROSSLEY, Edgbaston.

Rödgröd

(A Danish dish)

2 lbs. of red currants	2½ ozs. of sago meal, or if not obtainable,
½ lb. of raspberries	potato flour
½ lb. of sugar	

Squeeze the juice from the fruit in a cloth, add water to make up 2 pints in all. Press out the sago meal with a little of the juice, put the rest in a pan with the sugar and bring to the boil; add the sago meal and boil for 2 minutes. Stir for 2 minutes off the fire before pouring it into the glass or silver dish in which it is to be served.

Miss HELEN THEILMANN, Hull.

Sponge Crust Pudding

1 tablespoonful of butter	1 small teaspoonful of baking powder
1 small teacupful of flour	3 tablespoonfuls of sugar
1 egg	A pinch of salt

Beat butter and sugar to a cream, then beat egg into it, lastly add flour with baking powder, if too stiff add tablespoonful of milk. This mixture must be poured over boiling fruit into a pie-dish. Bake in a hot oven for a quarter of an hour.

Mrs. PHELPS, Scorton.

Cheese Pudding

Take equal quantities of breadcrumbs and grated cheese and mix with enough milk to make it about the consistency of porridge, season with pepper and salt and pour into a pie-dish. Place a few small pieces of butter on the top and bake a golden brown.

This pudding can be made richer by mixing with egg instead of milk, in which case the mixture should be made more liquid. Any pudding that is left will probably be solid when cold and can be made into another dish by cutting it into pieces, egging and breadcrumbing them and frying them in deep fat.

Miss MAY LAURENCE, Penrith.

Norfolk Dumplings (hard)

1 teacupful of flour makes 1 dumpling. Mix flour and water moderately stiff add a little salt. Drop into boiling water and let it boil 25 minutes (or more, it does not matter). Serve with beef or duck dripping, which may be thickened with a little flour, in a sauce-boat. A boiled batter pudding is always served with the dumplings. In old days they were always eaten before the meat.

Miss E. DOWSON, Geldeston.

Dinner and Supper Dishes

SOUPS

Barley Soup

1 pint of white stock	1 tablespoonful of Robinson's patent
¼ pint of milk	barley
2 tablespoonfuls of pearl barley	Seasoning to taste

Put stock which has been well flavoured with vegetables on to boil, when boiling add pearl barley and boil briskly for one and a half hours, then add Robinson's patent barley mixed with a little cold milk, and boil for ten minutes.

To make onions absolutely digestible, cut them open and put into boiling water with a pinch of carbonate of soda for 10 minutes, then throw water away.

Mrs. MORGAN, Claverdon.

Lettuce Soup

(*Zuppa-de-Erbe*)

Stock	Carrot
Sorrel	Onion
Endive	French roll
Lettuce	Parmesan cheese
Chervil	A little cream
Celery	

Boil the following vegetables in good stock for an hour: 2 small bunches of sorrel, a bunch of endive, 2 lettuces, a small bunch of chervil, a stick of celery, 1 carrot, 1 onion. All to be well washed and cut up small. Then put 2 pieces of toasted French roll into a tureen and then pour in the soup, after putting it through a hair sieve; last of all add a little cream. White stock should be used for this soup, and leeks give a more delicate flavour than onions.

Miss OTTER, Chelsea.

Sorrel Soup

Pick and thoroughly wash sorrel, lettuce and chervil, shred the whole, and put in a stewpan with a little butter, a little salt and pepper. Pop over the fire, stir with a wooden spoon till the sorrel is melted down, about 5 minutes; add about ½ oz. of flour, stir another 5 minutes; add the stock gradually, stirring all the time to prevent lumps from forming. Serve very hot, pouring the soup over small squares of toast.

Miss Dorothea M. Goldring, Claygate.

Soubise Soup

1½ pints of water	½ pint of milk
1½ ozs. of butter	5 ozs. of bread
1 yolk of egg	Pepper and salt
2 onions	

Put the onions, water, milk, butter and bread into a saucepan and boil until the onions are cooked, pass through a wire sieve; add the yolk of egg and simmer (but it must not boil) for a minute or two. To make it richer another yolk of egg and 1 gill of cream may be added.

Miss Warren, Hampstead.

FISH

Baked Sole with Cheese Sauce

Lay some fillets of lemon sole in a fireproof dish in which they can be served. Make a nice white sauce, well flavoured with grated cheese, and bake in a moderate oven for half an hour.

Miss Warren, Hampstead.

Fillets of Sole

Take some fillets of sole, put them in a dish and sprinkle some pepper, salt and lemon juice over them. Put the trimmings of the sole and the bones into a saucepan with pepper and salt, a little white wine (half a tumbler is plenty) and a few herbs, stew for half an hour and strain. Now put the fillets in a pie-dish with a trace of onion in the bottom; pour a little hot butter over them, then the stock, and put the dish in the oven or on the top of the stove. Cover it and cook gently, turning the pieces, then pour off the sauce into a saucepan and add butter and flour, and simmer until it thickens, pour back over the fish and let it go cold. After the fillets have lain a little while in the pepper and salt and lemon juice, they can be rolled in it and then put in the pie-dish, or in a fireproof covered dish, rather a low one for choice.

Mrs. Atkinson, Camberley.

Fish Cream

3 tablespoonfuls of light fish (whiting is best)	Seasoning
	Lemon
2 eggs	

Boil fish, bone and mash with fork, add well-beaten eggs and seasoning. Steam half an hour. Serve with sauce.   Mrs. ROBSON, Redditch.

Fish Pudding

¾ lb. of cold fish	¼ pint of milk
2 ozs. of butter	1 teaspoonful of parsley (finely chopped)
2 ozs. of breadcrumbs	Pepper and salt to taste
2 eggs	

Free the fish from all skin and bone, pound it in a mortar; mix with bread-crumbs and the butter melted, and the parsley and seasoning; *well* beat the eggs and stir in, and then the milk. Place in a basin or mould, well greased with dripping and covered with a well-greased paper, and put it into a saucepan half filled with water and steam for 1½ hours very gently. Serve with melted butter sauce into which a hard-boiled chopped-up egg has been lightly stirred. Can be served in separate mould.   Miss WARREN, Hampstead.

Lemon Soles in Potatoes

Cook fillets of soles in the following manner: Roll up, after seasoning them with cor-alline pepper, salt, butter, and squeeze of lemon; cook gently in oven, covered up with greased paper to prevent browning. Choose some nice shaped, *large* potatoes, roast in oven 1 hour, taking care to keep the skins whole and of good colour. Meanwhile prepare 2 lbs. (or 1 lb.) of spinach (as for entrée). When potatoes are done, take small cap off and scoop them out, leaving about the third of an inch of lining; now spread a lining of spinach evenly, next put roll of fish into potato, pour over good creamy sauce, sprinkle lightly with Parmesan cheese. Send hot to table.   Miss OTTER, Chelsea.

Stewed Oysters

50 oysters	½ cupful of breadcrumbs
1 pint of cream	1 pint of water
1 tablespoonful of butter	Salt and pepper

Drain the oysters in a colander and wash by pouring cold water over them. Cook the breadcrumbs and water together in a stewing pan for five minutes, add the oysters and then when boiling hot add the butter, cream, salt and pepper. Let the whole boil up once and then serve.

Miss MAUDE E. PARKIN, Goring-on-Thames.

Stuffed filleted Plaice

Pound either anchovies, or sardines, or carefully cooked kippered herrings, with a little butter, add a little sifted breadcrumb, milk, pepper and lemon peel. Spread thickly on raw fillets of plaice, roll up and fasten with a fine wooden skewer. Roll in egg and brown breadcrumbs and fry golden brown. Fry some parsley and serve very hot.

Mrs. SWANWICK, Manchester.

ENTRÉES AND MEAT

Cauliflower Soufflée

Prepare a soufflée dish in the usual way, place pieces of cauliflower and tomato at the bottom. Melt 1 oz. of butter in a saucepan, then mix in a heaped tablespoonful of flour; mix well, add teacupful of milk. Let this thicken on the fire, stirring all the time, then when a little cool add the yolks of 2 eggs, a little Parmesan cheese, pepper and salt to taste. Whip the whites of 3 eggs, mix all together, pour on the cauliflower and tomato in soufflée dish. Bake in a moderate oven 35 minutes.

Miss MILDRED MARTINEAU, Esher.

Creamed Eggs

Put some cream into the bottom of scallop shells and break an egg carefully into each, add salt and a little cayenne pepper and bake in the oven about 5 minutes. The eggs should be just set. The oven should not be too hot. Spoons are handed round with this entrée, as if properly done the eggs cannot be eaten with a fork.

Mrs. MORGAN WILLIAMS, Swansea.

Eggs à la Suisse

Spread the bottom of a dish with 2 ozs. of fresh butter, cover this with rather thin slices of fresh Gruyere or any other cheese; break 8 whole eggs upon the cheese without breaking the yolks, season with grated nutmeg, pepper and salt. Pour a gill of cream on the surface, strew the top with about 2 ozs. of grated cheese and put the dish in the oven to bake about 10 minutes. Pass a hot salamander over the top and serve on a flat dish with strips of toast (separately).

Mrs. GERARD DOWSON, Radcliffe-on-Trent.

Légumes de Deau

Carefully boil a good sized cauliflower, shred some carrots very fine and boil in salt and water for 10 minutes; peel and cook about 12 mushrooms in the oven for 10 minutes. Drain all the water from the cauliflower, which must be unbroken, and place in the centre of an entrée dish; cover with thick gravy sauce, then arrange the shredded carrots in each corner and place the mushrooms round the base. Serve very hot.

Mrs. S. A. P. KITCAT, Esher.

Peas à l'Italienne

Boil as many peas as will be wanted until they are quite soft, scramble as many eggs as will be wanted with plenty of butter and mix them with the peas. Keep the eggs from getting hard and serve very hot. A little more salt is wanted for this dish than in ordinary scrambled eggs, and some cayenne pepper should be added.

Mrs. MORGAN WILLIAMS, Swansea.

Tomatoes Farcies

6 small tomatoes (all of one size)	1 oz. of butter
6 mushrooms (chopped fine)	A little nutmeg
2 shallots	1 teaspoonful of brown sauce
1 onion	Browned breadcrumbs
2 ozs. of lean ham (cooked)	1 teaspoonful of Parmesan cheese
1 teaspoonful of parsley	Pepper and salt

Cut the centre of the tomatoes and without breaking them squeeze the juice or water out, season each one with a little pepper and salt. Put all the chopped ingredients into a sauté pan and stir over the fire with the butter until they are cooked, but not burnt; then add the brown sauce, the browned breadcrumbs, the nutmeg, and a little seasoning. Fill each tomato with the mixture, sprinkle over each a little Parmesan cheese with brown breadcrumbs. Bake about 10 minutes in a moderate oven.

Mrs. WALTER COHEN, Berkhamsted.

Brisket of Beef

A brisket of beef is delicious stewed in a pint of weak beer, or wine, with an onion stuffed with cloves, and a bunch of sweet herbs and pickled walnuts.

Mrs. PERCY WILLETT, Hove.

Chicken stuffed with Saccotosh

(American)

1 tin of corn	2 ozs. of cooked ham
1 onion	2 mushrooms
Parsley	Salt and pepper

Chop onion finely with parsley and mushrooms, cut ham into small dice, mix together. Stuff chicken, cook slowly, basting very frequently to ensure keeping chicken moist. Time, three-quarters of an hour. Chicken should be sewn up to prevent corn bursting out. Uncooked ham might be better than cooked. A good brown gravy poured over. (1 pinch of dried herbs might be added to stuffing.)

Miss OTTER, Chelsea.

Croquettes of Chicken

Melt 1 oz. of butter, put into it 1 dessertspoonful of flour and stir it well; add salt, pepper, and a very little nutmeg, 2 or 3 mushrooms, and a little parsley chopped up. Put all into a stewpan and stir for 2 or 3 minutes and add 4 spoonfuls of very good stock. Cut up some cooked chicken into small dice, and add a little ham, tongue, or bacon, and put into the sauce. Cook slowly for 20 minutes (do not let it boil or simmer), then take it all out of the stewpan and let it get cool. Then take some fine breadcrumbs, beat up 2 eggs in a soup plate; flour your pasteboard and make the mixture into short thick rolls, dip them into the breadcrumbs, then into the egg, then again in the breadcrumbs, and then fry them a rich brown.

Miss SHEPPARD, London.

Game or Poultry en casserole

Lay at the bottom of a fireproof covered dish some strips of bacon, an onion stuck with a clove, a carrot cut in strips, some celery, a bunch of herbs and 1 or 2 bay leaves. Then on this lay the bird cut up in joints. On the top of the bird lay some more strips of bacon and carrot, an onion, salt and pepper and pour in ½ pint of stock. Cook very slowly in the oven (3½ hours for a fowl, 2½ for smaller birds). At the last moment take out the upper layers of bacon, add a little thickening and a wineglassful of red wine.

A bird cooked in this way but omitting the bacon and the thickening and turned when cooked into a mould with 6 leaves of gelatine (less for a chicken) makes a nice supper dish. For this white wine (Chablis) is better than red, and the bird should be boned.

Miss MARY TANNER, London.

German Method of cooking Hare or Venison

Soak the hare or venison for 2 or 3 hours in a mixture made of half a tumbler of Chablis or any white wine (not sherry), 3 onions, 3 carrots, 2 laurel leaves, 12 peppercorns, 6 cloves. Then bake it in the mixture from 1 to 1½ hours. As soon as it is brown pour off the grease, take out the onions, etc., and add to the gravy ¾ pint of sour cream, and baste well with it.

Miss Mary Tanner, London.

Langue de Bœuf à la sauce piquante

If your ox tongue is salt, let it steep for 12 hours in water, changing it repeatedly. A "green" tongue is preferable. Put the tongue into a pan and cover with cold water; bring to the boil and let it simmer gently until it is very tender, 3 to 4 hours. Drain it and peel it while hot; cut away all the root, leaving the tongue neatly trimmed, with no bones. The root can be used for a stew, or minced and made into balls, etc. Slice and fry a golden brown, some carrots, turnips, onions and celery. Put 3 ozs. of butter into a bright pan and let it melt; take it off the fire and stir in 1 tablespoonful of flour. When perfectly smooth add gradually 1 pint of the liquor the tongue was boiled in and stir over a slow fire until thick. Put the sauce and the fried vegetables and the tongue all together in a pan (earthenware or aluminium is best) and simmer gently in the oven for an hour. Add 8 pickled walnuts and simmer for half an hour. Serve hot.

Mrs. Swanwick, Manchester.

Mutton en Casserole

Some cold meat	A little white sauce
Boiled rice	10 ozs. of grated cheese
A little onion juice	Salt and pepper
Brown gravy	

Butter and line a fireproof dish with a wall of boiled rice, free meat from fat and gristle and chop finely, season to taste; add a little onion juice and moisten very thoroughly with gravy, cover with a layer of rice. Put the lid on the dish and bake in a moderate oven for half an hour; then take off the lid, spread a layer of white sauce on top, sprinkle with grated cheese and return to the oven until nicely browned on top.

Mrs. Alfred Bucknill, Chelsea.

Pigeons "alla rustica"

2 pigeons	Slices of bacon
2 spoonfuls of oil	Small piece of butter
2 spoonfuls of vinegar	Pepper and salt

Take some small mild onions, peel them and soak in cold water for an hour. Put the pigeons wrapped in slices of bacon into a casserole, cover with the onions, add pepper, salt, a bit of butter and the oil and vinegar; cover closely and cook gently for about an hour.

Signorina E. B. Dobelli, Hampstead.

Tête de Veau en Tortue

Put a small calf's head (or half a large one) into cold water with salt and an onion stuck with cloves. Bring to the boil and then draw off and let simmer until tender, about 1½ hours. Drain and let it cool. Pick out the brains, cut the flesh off in pieces about 3 inches square, cut the tongue into slices about ½-inch thick. Fry the slices in hot fat (butter is best) until lightly brown. Put 3 ozs. of butter into a bright saucepan and let it melt; take it off the fire and rub in a tablespoonful of flour. When quite smooth and free from lumps, add 1 pint of the liquor the head was boiled in (cold) and stir over a slow fire until it is thick. Add the fried pieces and the brains and let the whole warm up very gently. Olives (stoned), mushrooms (fried), hard-boiled eggs, truffles and pistachio nuts (all sliced) and a few raw oysters should also be gently warmed in it and sippets of toast or croûtons should be placed round the dish in which it is served.

Mrs. Swanwick, Manchester.

West Country Game

Roast the birds and when cold cover with clotted cream and serve with lettuce hearts surrounding the bird.

Miss Sheppard, London.

SWEETS

Apricot Soufflée
(*Cold*)

Place a little apricot jam at the bottom of a soufflée dish. Then make a custard with the yolks of 3 eggs and ½ pint of boiling milk, then add 5 leaves of soaked gelatine and a little vanilla. When cold add ½ teacupful whipped cream, pour on to the jam in soufflée dish, put it aside till set; have some whipped cream ready to cover just before serving.

Miss MILDRED MARTINEAU, Esher.

A Supper Pudding

1 pint of milk	2 eggs
1 breakfast-cupful of breadcrumbs	Apricot preserve

Separate the whites and yolks of eggs; beat up yolks and add to milk and breadcrumbs in pudding dish, sweeten to taste and flavour with lemon, almond, or vanilla. Bake in oven to a light brown. Allow to cool. Whisk whites of eggs to stiff froth and then add one table-spoonful of castor sugar and whisk up again. Spread top of pudding with apricot jam (any preserve or marmalade will do) and over this spread the whisked whites of eggs; return to oven a few minutes to slightly brown top. This pudding is better cold.

Miss C. W. LOWRY, Chester.

Banana Cream with Brandied Cherries
(*Original*)

Make a Banana Fool with crushed bananas and cream and a very little sherry to taste. Serve cold, and hand round sauce of hot brandied cherries.

Miss OTTER, Chelsea.

Chocolate Cream
(*Excellent*)

¾ lb. of sugar	2 gills of milk
¾ oz. of gelatine	1 gill of water
3½ ozs. of chocolate	

Put all ingredients together in a jug and mix well, then put the jug in a saucepan of water on the fire, stirring occasionally till it boils; let it boil for 15 minutes, then stand the jug aside to cool. When the chocolate is nearly cold pour into a wetted mould.

Mrs. PHELPS, Scorton.

Fruit Juice Mould

Stew 1 lb. of fruit until it is quite tender. Pass it through a sieve. Add water to make 1 quart of juice. Mix 3 ozs. of cornflour with enough water to make it quite smooth. Bring the fruit juice to a boil and then stir in the cornflour. Simmer for about 10 minutes, stirring all the time. Sugar to taste should be added to the juice, not cooked with the fruit, to save waste.

Miss JULIA SHARPE.

Gateau d'Abricots

½ tin of apricots	1 tablespoonful of apricot marmalade
½ pint of whipped cream	2 slices of Genoese pastry, cut out with
1 tablespoonful of castor sugar	a round cutter
1 teaspoonful of vanilla essence	Chopped pistachio nuts
Savoy biscuits	¾ yd. of pale pink ribbon

Trim the Savoy biscuits neatly, as if for Charlotte Russe, brush the apricot marmalade over the Genoese pastry, place one slice on to a dish with a lace paper and stand the Savoy biscuits round it. Tie the ribbon around them to keep them in place. Cut the apricots each into 4 pieces, and reserve one-third for decorating. Mix the cream with the sugar and vanilla essence, and put half of it into a forcing bag with a rose pipe. Stir the apricots into the remainder and pour it into the biscuits, the cream on the top. Sprinkle with pistachio nuts.

Mrs. WALTER COHEN, Berkhamsted.

Ginger Cream

½ pint of cream	1 tablespoonful of ginger cut into
¼ oz. of gelatine, or rather more	small pieces
2 tablespoonfuls of syrup of	½ oz. of sugar
pre-served ginger	

Whip cream to stiff froth. Soak gelatine, pouring on to it just enough milk to cover it, when dissolved turn it very lightly into cream. Add sugar and ginger and put it into a cool place till nearly cold. Before it is set, pour it into a very slightly oiled mould. Turn it out and garnish with pieces of ginger and angelica.

Mrs. PHELPS, Scorton.

Pineapple, Peach or Apricot Pudding

½ tin of pine chunks (or of peaches)	2 ozs. of sugar
2 ozs. of flour	3 eggs
2 ozs. of butter	½ pint of milk

Cut the pine into small pieces and put into a pie-dish, with a little juice, and warm it. Take the other ingredients (except whites of eggs) and make as for a soufflée, when thoroughly cooked place over the pine. Beat the whites to a stiff froth, add 6 ozs. of castor sugar. When well mixed, put it roughly over the pudding. Sift over it a little sugar and set in the oven, not long enough to brown. Serve cold.

Mrs. ALFRED OSLER, Edgbaston.

Sponge Cake Shape

Take 4 penny sponge cakes, which must be very stale, and put them slowly through a sieve. Heat 3 sheets of gelatine, broken up, in ½ pint of milk; strain and let it go nearly cold. Whisk ½ pint of cream very stiff, mix the cake gradually to a cream, and add a little vanilla and brandy. Then pour in the gelatine and mix, and when nearly set put into a mould.

Mrs. ATKINSON, Camberley.

Stone Cream

Put a layer of apricot jam in an open glass or silver dish. Chop some almonds very fine and mix with as much cream as will make a thickness of about 1½ inches over the dish. Heat this with enough Russian isinglass to set it not too hard when cold, add ginger to taste and a few drops of lemon juice. It should not quite boil. Let it stand for a few minutes off the fire, and then pour it over the jam and set it to cool. This is good made with fresh milk or with half milk and cream. When cold cut almonds in strips and stick them on all over the surface. Some people do not like the chopped almonds through the cream. The lemon juice can be dropped over the jam if preferred but it is never mixed drop by drop with the cream. The quantities must be judged, for much more isinglass is wanted in summer than in winter. Gelatine may be used instead of isinglass, but is not *nearly* as nice.

Mrs. MORGAN WILLIAMS, Swansea.

SAVOURIES

Aberdeen Toast

4 oat cakes	1 oz. of butter
2 eggs	Cayenne
Bloater paste	

Make the oat cakes very hot, melt the butter, add one whole egg and the yolk of the other, the bloater paste and cayenne according to taste. Stir till thick, pile up on the hot biscuit, sprinkle with browned crumbs and serve at once.

Mrs. Robie Uniacke, Andover.

A Delicate Tomato Savoury

Divide the tomatoes in halves and take out a little of the centre of each; stuff with a mixture of finely chopped chickens' livers mixed with Parmesan cheese and breadcrumbs (finely chopped shallot fried in oil may be added by those who like this flavouring). Arrange the tomatoes on a baking-sheet, scatter over them bread-crumbs, grated cheese, and a little oiled butter. Bake in a steady oven and serve very hot.

Mrs. Robie Uniacke, Andover.

Cheese Aigrettes

¼ pint of cold water	1½ ozs. of Parmesan cheese
1 oz. of butter	2 eggs
2 ozs. of flour	Pepper, salt and cayenne

Put butter and water into a pan and allow to boil, then stir in flour and let it cook well, remove from the fire and add the cheese, then drop in the eggs one at a time, beat well, add seasoning. Drop teaspoonfuls of the mixture into hot fat, let them cook slowly a golden brown, and when done drain on a piece of soft paper and serve at once, piling high on a folded napkin.

Mrs. Phelps, Scorton.

Cheese Butterflies

2 ozs. of flour	1 yolk of egg
1½ ozs. of butter	Pepper and salt
2 ozs. of grated cheese	¼ pt. of cream to decorate

Rub the butter into the flour, add grated cheese and seasoning, mix to a stiff paste with yolk of egg, roll out on a floured board quite thinly. Cut into discs of two sizes, making an equal number of each size; cut the smaller discs into halves. Bake on a greased tin until a pale yellow. Upon the whole discs arrange the halves to represent butterflies' wings, keeping them in place with seasoned whipped cream; decorate with gherkins, capers and coralline pepper. The cream must be passed through a rose forcer.

Mrs. AUBREY DOWSON, Lapworth.

Cream Cheese Sandwich

Strain the juice from ripe red currants, mix it with new cream cheese to a soft paste, and spread on brown bread and butter.

Miss SHEPPARD, London.

Game Savoury

Mince cold game with some oysters, and add a tablespoonful of bread sauce, and season with pepper and salt. Cut thin slices of ham, spread the game and oysters on each slice, roll them up, place on a skewer and boil for 10 minutes Serve on hot toast with thick gravy.

Miss SHEPPARD, London.

Haddock Balls

Remove the skin and bones from a boiled (dried) haddock, mince and pound in a mortar with a little pepper, mace, etc., to taste. Add to this enough of a beaten-up egg to make a soft mixture, which is then rolled into little balls, dipped in the remains of the egg and breadcrumbs and fried in boiling fat. Serve very hot.

Mrs. ERIC CARTER, Edgbaston.

Indian Toast

2 eggs   1 oz. of butter
1 teaspoonful of anchovy essence   Fried bread
1 teaspoonful of curry powder

Melt the butter, and 1 whole egg and 1 yolk, the curry powder and the anchovy essence; stir till it thickens but do not let it boil. Pile up on the rounds of fried bread and serve very hot.

Mrs. ROBIE UNIACKE, Andover.

Pain Sauté

(*Chafing-dish Recipe*)

A slice of tin loaf ¾in. thick   2 tablespoonfuls of grated cheese
2 tablespoonfuls of butter   1 gill of cream
2 tablespoonfuls of finely minced ham   Cayenne pepper

Cut the crust from the bread, put the butter into a chafing-dish and when very hot lay the bread in it and fry till brown on both sides. Take it out and put in the cream, ham, cheese, and a pinch of cayenne. Stir together until very hot and spread the mixture on the toast.

Mrs. GARDNER, Edgbaston.

Vegetarian Dishes

Banana Croquettes

6 bananas	1 egg
½ teacupful of powdered sugar	2 teacupfuls of shredded wheat
Juice of 2 oranges	biscuit crumbs

Skin bananas, cut in halves crosswise; cut the ends straight, sprinkle with sugar and pour the orange juice over them. Stand in cool place for 1 hour, turning occasionally; roll in the egg and breadcrumbs. Fry in deep fat.

Miss IRENE DOWSON, Claygate.

Bavarois of Fruit

The fruit may be bottled or fresh. Just warm the fruit and put it through a hair sieve, add enough isinglass to make it set when cold; melt the isinglass before putting it to the fruit. Add a little cream and pour it into a large mould or small ones. Keep a little fruit back to make a syrup to pour round before serving. In summer it is improved by icing. This is especially good with damsons.

Mrs. C. W. EARLE, Cobham, Surrey.

Boboté

Take a thick slice of bread boiled in milk, then add 2 eggs and beat them up with the bread and milk. Make curry as follows: 2 onions (minced fine), 2 ozs. of butter, cook a good colour in a stewpan, then add curry paste or powder, some chutney and 1 apple; when properly flavoured add some protose, which must be cut very small, then boil for a quarter of an hour. Then add the eggs and bread and 3 teaspoonfuls of whisked Plasmon stock, and keep stirring. Squeeze half a lemon in the curry, the other half rub round the pie-dish; put all in well mixed, and bake half an hour.

Miss IRENE DOWSON, Claygate.

Chestnuts as a Vegetable

Boil 1 lb. of chestnuts, then skin them and put them into stock or gravy and simmer till tender. Flavour with lemon peel and thicken before serving.

If any of the above is left it can be rubbed through a sieve for soup and is most excellent.

Mrs. FAWCETT, London.

Mock Beef Rissoles

3 ozs. of fine rusk-crumbs	¾ pint of milk
2 ozs. of grated cheese	Whites of three eggs
3 ozs. of grated horse-radish	1 teaspoonful of made mustard

Mix well together the rusk-crumbs, cheese, mustard, pepper and horse-radish. Boil the milk and pour it over them and allow it to stand for 1 hour. Whip the whites of the eggs to a stiff froth and well mix all together, roll in fine rusk-crumbs and fry in boiling Albene. Serve very hot. If made into 9 rissoles the value of each one is 86 grains.

Miss NAPIER, Letchworth.

Rice Cutlets

½ pint of milk	Mace
1 oz. of rice (ground)	Onion
3 potatoes	Butter
Egg	

Put the milk on to boil, and thicken with rather more than 1 oz. of rice, to make a little stiffer than for rice mould; add a lump of butter, salt, a little grated onion, and a saltspoonful of mace, and let all cook together for 10 minutes, stirring frequently. Boil the potatoes and put through masher, and whilst hot add them to the rice or it will not set. Pour into flat dish to stiffen, and when quite cold cut into slices, roll in egg and breadcrumbs, fry, and serve with parsley sauce. The mixture must be quite stiff.

Mrs. E. ADAIR IMPEY, King's Norton.

Savoury Haricot Pie

Put a layer of cooked haricots in a buttered pie-dish, then a layer of carrot and turnip (previously par-boiled) to fill up the dish, pour in a little good gravy, cover with good white sauce well seasoned with made mustard, chopped parsley, etc., and coat thickly with breadcrumbs. Dot over with bits of butter, and bake from 20 to 30 minutes.

Many variations will suggest themselves—cauliflower, parsnip, vegetable marrow, sliced tomatoes, or beetroot, instead of the other vegetables.

Mrs. E. ADAIR IMPEY, King's Norton.

Sorrel and Asparagus Purée

Boil the sorrel very little in hot water with a little salt; lay it on a sieve under the tap and let lots of cold water run on it for several minutes, rub it through a hair sieve (this is the way to treat all green purées). Put the sorrel into an earthenware saucepan with good fresh milk and boil it together for about 10 minutes; before serving stir in a piece of butter the size of a walnut rolled in flour. Have ready some small asparagus cut in pieces and boiled till tender, stir it into the sorrel and serve hot. When asparagus is out of season it is very good with white French asparagus in tins.

Mrs. C. W. EARLE, Cobham, Surrey.

Spaghetti Macaroni

Boil some water in a pan, three-quarters full. Put into it half a teaspoonful of salt, a small onion, a piece of butter the size of a walnut, and while the water is boiling, ½ lb. of macaroni (the fine sort called spaghetti). Boil fast 5 minutes, then draw aside and simmer for an hour. Strain and put into a clean pan, with 5 tablespoonfuls of tomato pulp (no skin), 4 tablespoonfuls of milk and a pinch of cayenne pepper. Mix well. Add 2½ ozs. of Parmesan cheese (grated). Make all quite hot and serve quickly.

Miss LOWRY, Chester.

Spinach Gnocchi

Boil some spinach, drain well and pass through the sieve. To sufficient spinach for 2 people add half a cupful of thick cream, or better, some fresh cream cheese, and 2 eggs. Mix well and add a little flour if the paste is too wet. Make into little balls, roll them in flour and throw into quite boiling salted water. Boil a few minutes, when they will rise to the surface; as they do so, take them out, drain them well, and put them into a hot dish, scattering over them some grated Parmesan cheese and some bits of butter. When all are cooked, serve them quickly, as hot as possible. If liked, tomato sauce can be served in a tureen.

Signorina E. B. DOBELLI, Hampstead.

Vegetarian Pudding

Cover the bottom of a pie-dish with stoned raisins, next put a layer of bread in thin slices, thirdly a layer of sliced apples with a little sugar and nutmeg, then another layer of bread, fifthly, a layer of apples and raisins mixed, with sugar and nutmeg, and lastly a layer of bread. Fill up with boiling water, cover with another dish and stand in a tin with a little water in. Bake slowly in a cool oven for about 3 hours. The pudding should be eaten hot, and will not turn out of the dish.

Miss BIRD, ESHER.

Vegetarian Stock

The stock is made of the water in which vegetables, macaroni, spaghetti, or rice have been boiled, about 2 quarts. Cut up rather small all kinds of vegetables (except potatoes and cabbage), lettuces, carrots, turnips, celery, parsnips, onions, Jerusalem artichokes, leeks, a few white haricots and a bunch of sweet herbs; stalks, outside leaves, and peelings should be used. Let this boil slowly all day in a 2-quart saucepan, adding a little more of the cold vegetable or macaroni water to make up the necessary amount, skimming every 20 minutes or so for about 12 hours. An earthenware or enamel saucepan must be used for making vegetarian stock. Half an hour before dinner, strain the stock through a fine strainer and leave it to cool. If too light in colour add a little onion juice fried in butter; it ought to look quite clear and the colour of pale sherry. The vegetables strained from this soup are useless. This stock is the foundation for all soups and sauces and the greatest improvement to many dishes, it is the French *pot-au-feu* without the meat. England is the only country where outside leaves, stalks, shells and parings of vegetables are thrown away. From this stock vegetable soup is made by cutting up fresh vegetables, frying them in butter, and adding them to the stock, which by this time is nearly cold. For soups with macaroni, etc., the cereal must be boiled apart in a little of the vegetarian stock and more onion added. All soups are made more nourishing by grated Parmesan cheese handed at table.

Mrs. C. W. Earle, Cobham.

Salads and Sauces

American Fruit Salad

Line a salad bowl with lettuces. Peel and cut up peaches, oranges, grapes, melon, cucumber, celery, plums, etc., and place them in the bowl. Chop walnuts and scatter over the fruit. Pour mayonnaise sauce over the fruit. The walnuts may be omitted if preferred.

Miss F. E. Rendel, Charlwood, Surrey.

A nice Garnish for Cold Meat

Eggs boiled just hard, peeled and cut in two; on the halves lay a coiled anchovy previously washed in milk. Place little heaps of red radishes alternately with the eggs on the dish.

Miss Mary Tanner, London.

French Method of preparing Green Peas

Shell 2 lbs. of peas and place them in an earthenware casserole with lid. Put with them a lump of butter the size of a large walnut, 1 piece of lump sugar, 3 sprigs of parsley, 5 small spring onions, pepper and salt. Place the casserole with the lid on in a slow oven, and when the butter begins to melt stir the peas thoroughly in it until quite melted, then replace in the oven and leave for half-an-hour.

Miss Anne Stes, Sleights.

Oranges and Nuts Salad

Take 5 oranges, peel them, carefully removing all the white and transparent skin, and divide the yellow part into sections. Add to the oranges the white part of 12 walnuts, stir them together and place on lettuce hearts, separated (but not chopped up). Then make a dressing of 3 teaspoonfuls of oil, 1 of lemon juice, a very little cayenne and salt. This is a good salad to serve with game.

Miss Sheppard, London.

Salad

Take 1 lettuce, 2 tomatoes, half a cucumber, 2 apples, 2 pears, and 6 radishes. Cut all up and mix together. Sprinkle with salt and a little pepper. Pour on first 1 tablespoonful of vinegar and then 3 tablespoonfuls of salad oil. Take 1 hard-boiled egg and mix with 1 teaspoonful of mustard and 1 tablespoonful of oil. Pour mixture over salad and stir well. Add young onions to taste. This will give salad for 8 people.

Miss RAY COSTELLOE, Iffley.

Savoury Melon Salad

Peel a melon, cut into thin slices, arrange in layers in a glass dish, alternating with very thin slices of beetroot; sprinkle each layer with salt, pepper, olive oil and lemon juice, and serve with clotted cream.

Miss SHEPPARD, London.

Spinach Salad

Wash and boil 2 lbs. of spinach until tender, then drain; rub through a sieve when cold with salt, pepper, lemon juice, and stir in a spoonful of olive oil. Press into small moulds and set aside. Then cut 2 hard-boiled eggs into slices. Make a good mayonnaise sauce with the raw yolk of an egg, a spoonful of oil, a little tarragon vinegar, a few drops of mushroom ketchup, a little salt, and some thick cream. Turn out the spinach from the moulds, lay some egg slices over each, pour the sauce over, and lay slices of tomato all round.

Miss SHEPPARD, London.

Strawberry and Banana Sweet Salad

Cut bananas into slices and divide the strawberries in halves. Arrange them in alternate layers, sprinkle each layer with castor sugar, and pour a wineglassful of sherry over the whole, and lay small ratafias over the top and sides.

Miss SHEPPARD, London.

Sweet Melon Salad

Peel a ripe melon, take out seeds, and cut into thin slices, sprinkle with castor sugar, and pour over a glassful of white wine. Cover with whipped cream, flavoured with noyeau, and serve with wafer biscuits.

Miss SHEPPARD, London.

Winter Salad

Boil or steam 1 lb. of potatoes, cool and slice; slice 3 ripe tomatoes; stone 6 olives and slice; wash and slice 3 anchovies; boil 2 eggs hard and slice; add a tablespoonful of capers and a quantity of mayonnaise sauce made with nut oil. Mix thoroughly.

Mrs. SWANWICK, Manchester.

Hard Sauce

(American)

2 teaspoonfuls (level) of butter	Flavouring to taste (vanilla, almond,
2 tablespoonfuls (also level) of powdered sugar	or nutmeg)

Beat the butter to a cream, add the sugar, beating all till light and creamy, add flavouring and beat again. Pile lightly in cold place or on ice till cold and hard. Served with Christmas pudding.

Miss HELEN E. DOWNS, Brixton.

Merton Sauce

4 ozs. of butter	½ wineglassful of brandy
6 ozs. of white sugar	½ wineglassful of sherry

Beat the butter and sugar to a cream with a fork, and add gradually the brandy and sherry, beating until the mixture is perfectly stiff, and pile it high in the tureen. (Nice with Christmas plum pudding.)

Mrs. BUCKLEY, Edgbaston.

Tomato Sauce

4 lbs. of tomatoes	½ oz. of whole cloves
1 lb. of Demerara sugar	2 ozs. of whole white peppercorns
¼ lb. of common salt	1 pint of vinegar
3 ozs. of whole allspice	2 onions

Cut up the tomatoes, tie up the spices in a muslin bag, cut up onion, mix all ingredients together and boil in vinegar for 2 hours, stirring occasionally until the tomatoes become pulp. Rub through a wire sieve, and bottle.

Mrs. GARDNER, Edgbaston.

Butter Making

Things required:

1. Pans or leads
2. Skimmer and bowl
3. Cream cistern and stirrer
4. Cream can and strainer
5. Cream strainering (yards)
6. Butter muslin or old cloths
7. A kiver (oak)
8. Scales
9. A churn
10. Trenchers (2)
11. Glacialine (for hot climates)
12. Saltpetre, carbonate of soda, and bar of salt

Everything used in the dairy must be absolutely clean, and all pans, etc., must be scoured with sand, scalded and rinsed with cold water. Put carbonate of soda on all the bung corks. The cloths must be boiled every week and kept fresh and sweet smelling. Skim twice a day at regular hours, putting the cream into the cistern and stirring it, having previously put salt at the bottom and a teaspoonful of saltpetre. Churn on Thursdays and add salt to your cream on Mondays, Thursdays and Saturdays so that no salt is added to the cream you are about to churn after Monday. Put the cream in to the churn through strainering material. Churn till the butter comes. Draw off the butter-milk through the milk strainer. Put water in the churn and churn round to wash the butter thoroughly. Do this three times, drawing off the water. Take some brine water and strain it and put it in the kiver. Work the butter in the brine piece by piece, rolling each piece out twice, as quickly and lightly as possible, and up again. Empty off the brine and in a dry kiver work the water well out of every pound or two pounds of butter and shape each piece I⎺⎺⎺I. Then trencher each piece and it is done. You must be quick and firm and light, and there must be no holes, no cracks, and no water in good butter. Before commencing scald your hands and flour them, and rinse them in cold water, and you must keep your hands cool the whole time. *Scald everything you use.*

Miss Dorothea M. Goldring, Claygate.

Still-Room

BEVERAGES

Cider Cup

1 pint of bottled cider (sweet and sparkling)	1 liqueur glass of old brandy, or curaçoa
1 bottle of seltzer water	2 slices of lemon
	A lump of ice

Mrs. C. W. Dixon, Edgbaston.

Cinnamon Cordial

Infuse ¼ lb. of Ceylon cinnamon in 1 quart of good brandy for ten days, then add one drop of essence of orange peel, and one of cardamom, colour dark brown with caramel.

Miss Sheppard, London.

Cowslip Wine

Have a barrel well prepared and cleaned, a crock barrel preferred.

1 gallon of water	3½ lbs. of sugar (lump or Demerara,
3 qts. and 1 pt. of cowslip pips	the latter makes it a darker colour)
2 oranges	1 tablespoonful of balm
2 lemons	

To every gallon of water take 3½ lbs. of sugar and boil together for one hour, skimming it while boiling. Then let it cool. Have ready in the barrel 2 oranges, 2 lemons thinly peeled (pith and pippins removed) and sliced. Put in also half the peel of the oranges and the whole of the lemon peel. When the boiled water and sugar is nearly cool it can be put in the barrel and a piece of toast dipped in 1 tablespoonful of thick balm put in to work it. Stir it occasionally every day. When it has done hissing, which will be in about nine days, stop it down. If approved a bottle of brandy may be put in before it is stopped down. Bottle after six months, the wine improves by keeping in the bottles.

Mrs. Hugh Dixon, Tardebigge.

Damson Cordial

Put into a wide-mouthed jar 3 pints of gin, 2lbs. of candied sugar, 3lbs. of damsons. Shake jar occasionally to dissolve sugar, and in six weeks' time strain through jelly-bag, bottle and seal. Should be kept two years before using.

Mrs. C. W. DIXON, Edgbaston.

Sloe Gin

Made in the same way as Damson Cordial, but use 2½ lbs. of sugar to 3 lbs. of fruit.

Mrs. C. W. DIXON, Edgbaston.

Home-made Ginger-Beer

2 lbs. of lump sugar	½ oz. of cream of tartar
1 oz. of bruised ginger	2 lemons, juice and rind

Put all the above in an earthenware pan and pour on to it 1 gallon of boiling water, and when nearly cold add 1 oz. of German yeast soaked in a little cold water. Let it stand all night and then bottle it and tie the corks down firmly with string.

Miss OTTER, Chelsea.

Orange Liqueur

Stick half a dozen cloves into a Seville orange, put it in an earthen jar with 1½ pints of best brandy (or gin) and leave it for a month. Boil 1 lb. of loaf sugar quickly with ½ pint of water, pour it into the brandy and leave it for another month. Filter the liqueur through filtering paper (from any chemist), pour it into bottles, cork and seal and store for use.

Mrs. C. W. DIXON, Edgbaston.

Stinger

(A cold-weather temperance drink. Not for children)

2 lbs. of loaf sugar	½ oz. of tartaric acid
½ oz. of essence of cayenne	3 lemons, rind and juice
½ oz. of essence of ginger	2 quarts of boiling water

Peel the lemons and boil the rind for 10 minutes in ½ pint of water. Strain and add to the rest of the ingredients and 2 quarts of boiling water. Stir until it is all dissolved. This makes about 4 bottles of concentrated essence, to be taken in the proportion of about 2 tablespoonfuls to a tumbler of hot water.

Mrs. SWANWICK, Manchester.

Strawberry Sherbet

(American)

1 quart of strawberries	1 tablespoonful of orange-flower water
3 pints of water	¾ lb. of white sugar
1 lemon, the juice only	

The strawberries should be fresh and ripe. Crush to a smooth paste and add the rest of the ingredients (except the sugar) and let it stand 3 hours. Strain over the sugar, squeezing the cloth hard, stir until the sugar is dissolved; strain again and set in ice for 2 hours or more before you use it.

Miss EVELYN ATKINSON, Camberley.

PRESERVES

Apple Butter

(American)

(Economical, as it uses up all apple, peelings and pulp.)

Simmer peelings and pulp with enough water to cover. Strain through coarse colander, measure in cup, and add *equal* amount of sugar (soft sugar). Add lemon juice if liked. Yellow part of rind could have been previously simmered with pulp. Evaporate down by standing on side of stove uncovered, simmering till thick enough to spread on bread. Grape Butter can be made in same way, using skins and all.

Miss HELEN E. DOWNS, Brixton.

Damson Cheese

To every pound of fruit pulp allow ½ lb. of sugar. Put the damsons into a preserving pan and simmer until they are soft, occasionally stirring them, then put them through a coarse sieve; put back into the preserving pan with sugar in the above proportion, having carefully weighed the pulps in juice. Stir the sugar in well and simmer 2 hours. Skim, then boil the preserve quickly for ½ hour, or until it looks firm in the spoon, put it quickly into earthenware moulds, cover with oiled paper. A few of the stones may be cracked and the kernels boiled with the damsons, which is a great improvement.

Miss IRENE DOWSON, Claygate.

Dried Apricot Jam

2 lbs. of dried apricots	3 ozs. of bitter almonds
7 lbs. of sugar	7 pints of water

Cover the apricots with the water, and let them soak for 48 hours. Put into the pan with sugar and blanched and split almonds and boil quickly for about an hour.

Mrs. PHELPS, Scorton.

Lemon Curd

Take 4 eggs, beat them well, then the rind of 2 lemons grated, and the juice, 1 lb. of loaf sugar, ¼ lb. of butter. Set over a slow fire. Stir till all is as thick as honey. Do not let it boil.

Mrs. DOWSON, Gorleston-on-Sea.

Madeira Marmalade

1 doz. of bitter oranges	½ doz. sweet oranges
3 lemons	

Slice the fruit very thin, cutting each one in quarters, and taking out the pips. To every pound of sliced fruit and pulp add 3 pints of water. Let it stand for 24 hours, and then boil until the chips are quite tender. Let it stand again for 24 hours. Weigh the boiled fruit, and to every pound of fruit add 1 lb. of sugar and boil again from half-an-hour to an hour, as the marmalade should be clear and well jellied. A wineglassful of whiskey can be added during the last boiling if desired.

Miss ETHEL JACOBS, Hull.

Orange Marmalade

(*Very good indeed*)

Cut the oranges as thin as possible, taking out the pips. To every pound of fruit add 3 pints of cold water, let it stand 24 hours; then boil until perfectly tender, and stand till the following day. Weigh the fruit again, and to every pound put 1½ lbs. of loaf sugar. Have it on large meat dishes so that the sugar is distributed all over the fruit. Let it stand so for 2 or 3 hours. Then put it in the preserving pan on the fire, but be very careful that all the sugar melts into the fruit before the whole boils. Let it boil till it becomes transparent and jellies, probably about ½ to ¾ hour.

Mrs. ATKINSON, Camberley.

Raspberry Jam

To every 1 lb. of raspberries add 18 ozs. of sugar. Break up all well together. Let it stand for 2 days and then let it come *very slowly* to the boil. Remove from the fire as soon as it boils, and cover while hot. This recipe preserves the flavour of the fresh fruit.

Mrs. FAWCETT, London.

Red Currant Jelly without Boiling

Squeeze out the juice of the raw currants by small handfuls through a piece of muslin into a basin. Take the weight of the juice and weigh out the same quantity of powdered white sugar. Gradually stir in the sugar a little at a time, taking ½ hour to get it all in. Then continue stirring slowly for ½ hour longer. Put into pots and cover over next day.

Miss KING, Esher.

Rum Butter

(Old Lancashire Recipe as made by Mrs. Hendley of Coniston)

1½ lbs. of sugar   ½ wineglassful of good rum
1 lb. of fresh butter

Melt the butter in a bowl, then add the sugar and mix to a thick cream, adding the rum according to taste. When cold it should be set, and is eaten as a preserve. For those who do not like the flavour of rum ½ wineglassful of lemon juice may be substituted, or it may be flavoured with essence of vanilla or almond. This recipe has been used in the lake district for generations, on all family festivities, at christenings or on Christmas Day.

Miss EVELYN ATKINSON, Portesbery Hill, Camberley.

Vegetable Marrow Jam

Cut marrow up into large pieces, and put 1 lb. of sugar to 1 lb. of marrow, and let it stand for 24 hours, having added lemon juice and rind to flavour, and bruised ginger (this to be added while boiling). Boil for 2 or 3 hours until it becomes of a good golden colour.

Mrs. AUBREY DOWSON, Lapworth.

To Preserve Pears

Peel the pears. Stew gently, with ⅔ claret and ⅓ water, and half the weight of pears in loaf sugar, a few cloves, and candied peel cut in thin strips. Let the pears be soft, but not mashed. Add a few drops of cochineal to the syrup. They will keep for months if put in wide-mouthed bottles and closely covered and tied down.

Miss Dorothea M. Goldring, Claygate.

PICKLES

Chutney

2 lbs. of brown sugar	1 lb. of onions
½ lb. of sultanas	2 lbs. of apples
½ lb. of currants	2 qts. of vinegar
½ lb. of dates	Sliced mango

Chop these ingredients very finely and put into the cold vinegar, and boil steadily until quite soft. Have ready to mix in a pennyworth of cayenne, 2 ozs. of mustard, 2 ozs. of salt, 1 oz. of ground ginger. Let it all boil up again for a good hour, use a wooden spoon for stirring. When cold it is ready for use.　　Miss Mary Johnstone, Camberley.

Tomato Chutney

Wipe 4 lbs. of ripe tomatoes with soft cloth, remove stalks and break in half and place in preserving pan. Wipe 1 lb. of cooking apples, cut them in quarters and add to the tomatoes. Slice up 6 small onions and add to fruit in pan, together with ¼ lb. of salt, 1 oz. of crushed mustard-seed, ½ oz. of grated ginger, 1 small teaspoonful of cayenne pepper and 5 gills of malt vinegar. Place over moderate heat. When fruit begins to soften, stir in 1 lb. of moist sugar. Boil till ingredients are reduced to a pulp, and rub through a coarse hair sieve into a basin. Leave for 24 hours at least before bottling.　　Mrs. G. Farewell Jones, Mitcham.

Green Tomato Pickle

12 lbs. of tomatoes	1 oz. of mustard-seed
3 lbs. of onions	1 oz. of peppercorns
4 lbs. of treacle	½ oz. of chillies (small)
5 quarts of vinegar	½ oz. of cloves

Cut tomatoes in small pieces and sprinkle with salt; let stand in a basin for at least 12 hours, then throw away the water that comes from them. Cut the onions small (don't salt). Heat vinegar, add mustard mixed with some vinegar, add treacle and spices, bring to the boil, add tomatoes and onions. Boil for 20 minutes. Fit to eat directly it is cold.

Miss Dorothea M. Goldring, Claygate.

Home-made Baking Powder

3 ozs. of tartaric acid	4 ozs. of rice flour
4 ozs. of carbonate of soda	

To be well mixed together.

Mrs. Aubrey Dowson Lapworth.

Mutton Ham

To cure

A leg of mutton, 8 lbs., no tail	½ lb. of brown sugar
1 lb. of salt	Allspice and pounded herbs
10 ozs. of saltpetre	

Rub in the salt, saltpetre and sugar, rub 2 or 3 days, then rub in allspice and pounded herbs. Work and turn for 3 weeks, then hang up in larder and let it drip dry. No smoking or bag needed if done at time of year when there are no flies.

To boil Ham

Soak all night. Boil 1½ to 2 hours. Let it lie in water till going cold.

Mrs. Gayton, Merstham.

Potted Hare

1 lb. of scalloped veal	1 hare or 2 small rabbits
½ lb. of sausage meat	

Take off the fillets and as many pieces as you can. Carefully remove the liver and the kidneys. Put to boil in a saucepan with about 4 tumblerfuls of water, all the remains of the hare or rabbit, head, etc., and boil well. Mince fine 2 or 3 onions, a bunch of parsley, strip 2 or 3 branches of thyme, ½ teaspoonful of allspice, the liver of the rabbit or hare, the sausage meat, all well minced, salt and pepper. Mix all this with the gravy made from the remains of the hare and a wineglassful of brandy. The earthenware pottery pot must have a lid with a hole in it to let out the steam. Garnish the pot with a few slices of bacon fat, some slices of scalloped veal. Spread over with a spoon the mixture of minced meat, filling in all gaps, then add slices of hare or rabbit, divide the kidney and put in here and there, go on doing this until the pottery pot is full. Press it all down well and put on the top a few slices of bacon, fix the lid down tight. Wet a little flour with some water to make a thick paste and put round the slit of the lid with your finger. Put to cook in the oven for 4 or 5 hours. To be eaten cold. If you wish to turn out, soak the pot in hot water. Keeps for some time.

Madame Alexandre Touraine, France.

To Preserve Eggs

1 part waterglass (silicate of soda) to 10 parts of water (by weight)

Boil 2 or 3 quarts of water and pour over the waterglass, stirring till thoroughly mixed. Then add as much water as required. When quite cold it is ready for use. The eggs should be dropped in as soon as possible after they are laid and they should not be more than 12 hours old. Eggs preserved in waterglass keep good for a year. If they are to be boiled in their shells, the shells should be punctured top and bottom before they are put into hot water, otherwise they are apt to burst.

Mrs. SWANWICK, Manchester.

To Spice Beef

For a piece of beef 10 lbs.:

¼ lb. of saltpetre	4 tablespoonfuls of mixed spice
¾ lb. of common salt	½ lb. of brown sugar

Place the beef in a crock pan, sprinkle the saltpetre well into all the crevices and rub in with the hand until it dissolves. Then sprinkle the other ingredients one at a time all over the beef and rub. The beef must be well rubbed and turned each day and the liquor which is made by the dissolving sugar must be ladled over the beef every day before rubbing. The beef must remain in the pan for 14 days, or longer if very highly spiced beef is preferred. Then wash and boil in the ordinary way.

Miss WALFORD, Kingswood.

To Pickle Beef Tongues

Tongue, 7 to 8 lbs.	1 oz. of saltpetre
1 oz. of black pepper	½ oz. of brown sugar
½ lb. of bay salt	½ lb. of treacle

Trim off the gullet, rub over the tongue a handful of salt and let it drain on a dish until the following day (this liquor to be thrown away), rub it well with the saltpetre, sugar and pepper mixed together, put into the pickling tub and leave 2 days more, then rub with the bay salt, dried and pounded; at the end of 3 days more, pour over it the treacle and leave it in this pickle for a fortnight, turning and basting every day. It can then be used at once or if drained and hung in a dry, airy place will keep a long time, but in that case will need to be soaked in tepid water 3 or 4 hours before boiling. If the pickle is boiled up a piece of unsalted silver-side or brisket of beef may be put into it and if turned and basted daily for a fortnight will be nicely flavoured.

Miss WARREN, Hampstead.

SWEETMEATS

Cocoanut Ice

Four cups of white soft sugar level with the top of the cup (breakfast-cup size), 2 cups of dessicated cocoanut as full as would be filled for a usual cup of tea, 1 cup of milk filled to same height. Pour all into a saucepan together, stir well till it boils; it ought not to take longer than 10 minutes. Then remove the spoon, stirring only occasionally to prevent burning, keep on fire after it boils 3 or 4 minutes. Take the saucepan off and stand it in a basin of cold water, and beat contents with a fork until thickish (do not let it get too thick, it should pour out quite easily). Turn out on to a buttered dish and spread smoothly about half an inch thick. Do a second batch in the same way, but colour this, on taking it off the fire, with a little cochineal. Sometimes the first batch turns a little brown, then colour *that* with the cochineal and be more careful with the second batch. (A great deal depends on the sugar used.)

Miss HELEN E. DOWNS, Brixton.

Cream Toffee

Ingredients: 1 lb. of soft or castor sugar, butter the size of a walnut, 1 tin of condensed milk ("Ideal" unsweetened is to be recommended), a wine-glass of water, flavouring essence. A little vinegar can be added for those who think toffee too sweet. A handful of walnuts added just before taking off the fire makes a good sweetmeat.

Put the butter in the saucepan (copper if possible) and melt. Add the sugar gradually, and a little water (and vinegar if liked) now and then to prevent burning. Some sugars require more water than others. Add the milk gradually and stir until the mixture comes well away from the sides of the pan. Add flavouring and nuts, if wished, a few minutes before taking off the fire. Pour into tins, and cut in squares when slightly set. Time: ½ hour.

Mrs. VINCENT, Camberley.

Marchpane

(Rather expensive and troublesome, but very good)

1 lb. of recently shelled almonds, throw into boiling water for minute to loosen skins. Throw into cold water and rub off skins. When dry bray in a mortar, add 2 teaspoonfuls of orange-flower water (or more, to taste), to ½ lb. weight of the blanched

almonds. Pound to the consistency of oil. (This takes a long time and a heavy hand.) Add an equal quantity of confectioner's white sugar, and put on stove in an earthen-ware pot (an emptied jam-pot will do), inside a saucepan of boiling water. Stir and press occasionally with a wooden spoon. Work until it ceases to cling to the sides of the pot. Take away from fire and cool. Lay out on a pastryboard and knead into it as much more sugar as it will take up (about ½ lb.). Roll into a long strip and cut up into lozenge- or heart- or any fancy-shaped pieces. Lay on plate to dry slowly in cool oven.

Miss HELEN E. DOWNS, Brixton.

Preserved Orange Balls

Take some dried orange peel and soak for 2 days, changing the water frequently to remove the bitter taste. Then boil, and when boiled weigh the peel, taking an equal weight of coarse moist sugar. Put the peel through a mincing machine, and when minced lay the mixture on a porcelain plate or slab, and mix with just enough water to make it into balls the size of a large walnut.

FRAU WILBRANDT, Heiligenblut, Carinthià.

Simply-made Cream for Date-Creams

Pour the *white* of 1 egg, *not* beaten, into a spoon for the purpose of measuring, turn into basin and add as much cold water as there was white of egg measured in the same spoon, mix thoroughly but *do not beat*. Stir in enough confectioner's icing sugar to make it the consistency of dough (about 1 lb.). Flavour with vanilla (a teaspoonful, or to taste). Fill prepared dates or prunes, and set in a warm (not hot) place to harden. Almonds or walnuts can be cased in this.

Miss HELEN E. DOWNS, Brixton.

Toffee

¼ lb. of butter	1 cup of water
1 lb. of brown sugar	1 teaspoonful of vinegar
1 cup of treacle or golden syrup	

Melt the butter in a saucepan, add the sugar (drawing the pan off the fire), and the water. Stir well and put on the fire again. Add the treacle or syrup, boil for about 15 minutes, stirring all the time. Pour a few drops into cold water and if they harden at once the toffee is ready. Add the vinegar and stir in well, then pour into buttered tins and leave to harden.

Miss JANET HAMILTON THOMSON, Highgate.

Turkish Delight

1 qt. packet of Nelson's gelatine soaked 2 to 3 hours in ¾ cup of cold water (breakfast cup). Mix in saucepan 2 lbs. of soft white sugar and 1 cup of boiling water. Add the ready soaked gelatine, stir all the time over the fire till it comes to the boil, let it boil 15 minutes, stirring all the time. Flavour with 1 large teaspoonful each of lemon and vanilla flavouring (as sold in bottles for cooking purposes), mixed in *after* it comes off the fire. This is to be poured into 2 (ready buttered) soup plates. It looks well to colour contents of one with a few drops of cochineal. Remove any scum. Let it stand in cold place 24 hours, cut into squares on a pastryboard sprinkled with *icing sugar*. Roll squares in icing sugar and pack lightly into little paper baskets or ornamented paper trays.

Miss HELEN E. DOWNS, Brixton.

SCENTS, POT-POURRI

Cologne Water

(*Fine. American Recipe*)

1 drachm of oil of lavender			50 drops of tincture of musk		
1	”	”	bergamot	8 ”	oil of cinnamon
2	”	”	lemon	8 ” ”	cloves
2	”	”	rosemary	1 pint of alcohol	

Miss EVELYN ATKINSON, Camberley.

Cologne Water

60 drops of oil of lavender			60 drops of orange-flower water	
60	”	”	bergamot	1 pint of alcohol
60	”	”	lemon	

Cork and shake well.

Miss EVELYN ATKINSON, Camberley.

Green Herb Bags

(For preventing moths)

½ lb. of dried rosemary   ¼ lb. of dried thyme
½ lb.   ”   mint   ¼ lb.   ”   Tansy
2 tablespoonfuls of cloves

Mix and store in a well closed box. Make small square sachets of green checked muslin, about 5 inches square is a good size, and fill with the mixture. Or the powder may be scattered among furs, blankets, etc. Adapted from an old recipe.

Miss Evelyn Atkinson, Camberley.

Lavender Water

To 1 part of pure distilled lavender oil add 40 parts of alcohol.

Mrs. C. W. Dixon, Edgbaston.

Bread, Cakes, Scones and Biscuits

Beef Bread

2 lbs. of white flour (stone milled if possible)
½ lb. of best rump steak
½ oz. of German yeast
1 saltspoonful of salt
1 saltspoonful of castor sugar
Water

Mince very fine some fresh rump steak, best quality, with no fat or gristle or skin, so as to make exactly ½ lb. when minced. Dry and sift the flour and set it in a large pan to warm. Rub the minced, raw beef into the dry flour as lightly as possible, but so as to mix it very completely. Rub the yeast and sugar into a breakfastcupful of tepid water (new-milk temperature). Make a hole in the flour and pour the yeasty water in, stirring a little of the flour in so as to make a mixture like thick cream in the middle of the pan, with a wall of dry flour round. Lay a cloth over the top of the pan and set it in a warm place for an hour. Add the salt and as much tepid water as is required to make a stiff dough. It should leave the pan clear. Lift the dough on to a board and knead lightly but thoroughly for 10 minutes. Make into a ball and put back in the pan, score it with a sharp knife and set to rise in a warm place with a cloth over the top for 2 hours. It should swell to double its original size. Knead up quickly and lightly and make into loaves, large or small according as you prefer crumb or crust. Stand for 10 minutes on a baking sheet in a warm place. Bake. The oven should be quick to begin with and slow later. This sort of bread should bake rather longer than ordinary bread, it tastes and looks like fine brown bread, it keeps moist and good for a week or 10 days and makes nourishing sandwiches. When stale it can be boiled with vegetables to make an excellent soup. One of the great secrets of bread-making is to have your dough, etc., the right temperature, warm but not hot, also to knead with a light springy touch.

Mrs. SWANWICK, Manchester.

Breakfast Bread

1 lb. of flour
1 cup of cream
A small pinch of salt
½ teaspoonful of carbonate of soda

Mix all these together, roll out an inch thick, cut into small cakes, bake 10 minutes. Serve hot. Great care needed not to let them burn.

Mrs. PHELPS, Scorton.

Breakfast Rolls

2 lbs. of best pastry flour	1 pint of milk
1 oz. of German yeast	A little water and salt added
Rather more than 1 oz. of butter	

Melt the butter, warm the milk, mix and add to the yeast which has been stirred with a large teaspoonful of sugar, till liquid, pour on the flour and mix thoroughly. Cover with a cloth and set in a warm place until it rises well up (an hour). Turn on a board, well knead and roll out thick, stamp in rounds, set them to rise again, for 5 or 10 minutes. Bake in a moderate oven.

Miss G. E. SOUTHALL, Edgbaston.

Buttermilk Bread

(*American recipe*)

1 pint of butter-milk heated to scalding, stir in, while it is hot, enough flour to make a tolerably thick batter, add ½ gill of yeast and let it rise 5 or 6 hours. If you make it overnight you need not add the yeast but put in, instead, a tablespoonful of white sugar. In the morning stir into the sponge a tablespoonful of soda dissolved in hot water, a little salt and 2 tablespoonfuls of melted butter. Work in just flour enough to enable you to handle the dough comfortably, knead well, make into loaves and let it rise until it is light. Very wholesome bread.

Mrs. ALFRED BOOTH, Liverpool.

Irish Sweet Loaf

1 lb. of dough	1 or 2 teaspoonfuls of sugar
1 egg (well beaten)	Butter, size of a walnut

Bake in moderate oven. Can be eaten hot and buttered, or cut as cold bread and butter.

Mrs. GRANT, Camberley.

Bachelor's Lunch Cake

Beat 1 lb. of soft sugar into ½ lb. butter for 15 minutes. Mix 1 pint of buttermilk with 2 teaspoonfuls of carbonate of soda, and 1 teaspoonful of tartaric acid. Add both sugar and butter, mix in 1 lb. of raisins with 1½ lbs. of flour, 1 oz. of mixed spice and 2 ozs. of finely chopped orange peel. Mix all together and bake in moderate oven for two hours.

Mrs. WHITWELL, Esher,

Butter Cakes

1 lb. of flour	1 egg
¾ lb. of butter	1 teaspoonful of cinnamon
¾ lb. of silver castor sugar	A few chopped almonds

Rub the butter well with the flour as for making pastry. Then put in the other ingredients, mixing all into a stiff paste with the beaten egg. Let it stand for half-an-hour in a cool place, then roll out and cut with a round cutter. Bake the cakes on flat tins in a quick oven for 15 minutes. Some blanched and split almonds can be put on the top of each cake. The butter should be soft when rubbed in the flour or it will not mix.

Miss ETHEL JACOBS, Hull.

Chocolate Cake

½ lb. of grated chocolate	6 ozs. of white castor sugar
½ lb. of butter	1 teaspoonful of baking powder
¼ lb. of flour	4 eggs
2 ozs. of ground rice	

Beat the butter to a cream. Add to it the sugar, then beat in the eggs one by one until each is well mixed. (Do not put in the next if the mixture seems to curdle.) Put a dessertspoonful of flour into it—the flour should be sifted through a sieve. The grated chocolate should be stirred in last with the exception of the baking powder. The mixture should then be poured into a well-buttered paper-lined tin. This cake takes from an hour to an hour and a half to bake. It should be put into a very quick oven, and the oven should not be opened for 20 minutes after it is put in. If it seems done, try it with a skewer.

Miss E. ROWAN HAMILTON, Shankill.

Fluffy Sponge Cake

¾ lb. of loaf sugar	6 fresh eggs
½ lb. of finest Austrian (or potato) flour	Flavouring

Before beginning the cake, line a large round cake tin with well-buttered paper. Get your oven rather hot. Put the sugar to melt over a gentle fire with half a teacupful of hot water. Don't stir more than you can help. Draw off when it has become a syrup and add the flavouring you prefer. Vanilla essence is a great favourite. Caramel, chocolate or coffee are all good, but it is necessary that they should be *strong*, otherwise the effect is sickly. If no flavouring is used, the eggs give their full flavour and some people like this best. Whisk the eggs for two or three minutes in a large bowl (the bowl must be at least a foot across). When the syrup has cooled considerably, whisk it gradually into the eggs and go on whisking for 20 minutes. You must never stop and it is important to raise the batter very high so as to ærate it very completely. Pour the batter into the tin and put at once into the oven. Do not open the door for a ¼ of an hour. The oven should then be allowed to slow down somewhat (but do not open the door oftener than necessary), and after half-an-hour a piece of white paper should be laid on the top of the lining paper (which should project considerably above the tin). Time to bake, about one hour. Test in the usual way with a long pin. It should be a light golden-brown colour, and to keep it fairly level it should be turned round once or twice in the baking. Leave it in the tin for 5 minutes after it comes out of the oven and then shake out and stand in a sieve to cool, in a warm kitchen. Cut with a very sharp knife.

Mrs. SWANWICK, Manchester.

Harvest Buns

When making bread take some of the dough, make into buns with some currants, sugar, lard, and a little butter. To be eaten with butter.

Miss E. DOWSON, Geldeston.

Luisen Gebäck

(*German*)

½ lb. of flour	¼ lb. of butter
¼ lb. of almonds, chopped up small *with* skin	½ lb. of white sugar
	3 eggs

Mix butter and eggs together till creamy. Add sugar and flour gradually, then the almonds. Mix well and roll lightly and cut into shapes. Bake till pale brown in moderate oven.

Mrs. C. W. DIXON, Edgbaston.

Orange Cake

The weight of 2 eggs in butter, granulated sugar and good self-raising flour, 1 large or 2 small oranges; grate the rind on the sugar and with the fingertips rub them together. Cream the butter, add the sugar and flour, a spoonful at a time, well beating until all are used. Bake in a very slow oven for an hour or longer, test with knitting pin and turn out carefully. Mix half a cupful of castor sugar to a stiff paste with a little of the orange juice and spread smoothly on the top of the cake when cold.

Miss G. E. SOUTHALL, Edgbaston.

Plätzchen

(*German*)

3 eggs

½ lb. of flour

½ lb. of sifted sugar

Grated peel of 1 lemon

Stir eggs and sugar and add flour and lemon for 20 minutes. Put blobs of the paste on to a paper-covered tin and bake ¼ hour to a delicate buff colour.

Mrs. C. W. Dixon, Edgbaston.

Potato Cake

(*Cornish recipe*)

1 lb. of potatoes, boiled, mashed
very fine

½ lb. of flour

½ lb. of suet

1 egg

½ lb. of sultanas

Mix with milk and bake in flat cakes.

Miss Alice Nöel Herbert Wright, Solihull.

Scotch Short Cake

1 lb. of flour

½ lb. of butter

6 oz. of white sugar

Work the butter to a cream, stir in the sugar, and then by degrees all the flour, and roll out about an inch thich. Cut in squares and ornament with caraway comfits and candied peel. Bake till light brown.

Mrs. C. W. Dixon, Edgbaston.

Simnel Cake

2½ lbs. of butter, 2 lbs. of sifted sugar. Beat together till they become a cream, then break in, one by one, beating all the time, 20 fresh eggs. Stir in gently 2 lbs. of fine flour, 2½ lbs. of currants, 1½ lbs. of citron and 8 ozs. of orange peel, but cut up fine. Have ready separately 2 lbs. of sweet almonds, ½ lb. of bitter almonds, blanched and beaten as fine as possible, with a wineglassful of brandy and a small tablespoonful of vanilla. Add to this 2½ lbs. of finely sifted sugar and mix into a paste with 6 fresh eggs well beaten. Have a large baking tin lined with a single paper, into which put about half of the fruit mixture. Cover with wafer paper, then gently spread with half of the almond paste, wafer paper again and the rest of the fruit mixture, wafer paper again, and the rest of the almond paste. Bake in a quick oven for 6 hours. The almond mixture should be made the day before. The outside of the tin must be wrapped round with many thicknesses of white paper, also underneath the tin on which the cake stands, to prevent it burning.

Mrs. C. W. Dixon, Edgbaston.

Snow Cake

1 lb. of arrowroot	Whites of 6 eggs
½ lb. of white pounded sugar	Flavouring to taste: essence of almond,
½ lb. of butter	vanilla or lemon

Beat the butter to a cream, stir in the sugar and arrowroot gradually, at the same time beating the mixture. Whisk the whites of the eggs to a stiff froth, add them to the other ingredients and beat well for 20 minutes. Put in the flavouring, pour the cake into a buttered mould or tin, and bake in a moderate oven from 1 to 1½ hours.

Miss CONSTANCE SILLEM, Esher.

Mrs. Mildren's Cornish Sponge Cake

(*Most excellent*)

The weight of 3 eggs in castor sugar and 2 eggs in flour. Mix the 3 eggs and sugar together, the eggs not previously beaten, and gradually sift in the flour, to which has been put 1 teaspoonful of baking powder, and beat all together for ½ hour. Bake in a slow oven 20 minutes to ½ hour.

Mrs. GAYTON, Merstham.

Swiss Almond Cake

6 fresh eggs	¼ lb. of castor sugar
¼ lb. of almonds, ground very fine with the skins left on	The grated rind of an orange

Beat the yolks with the sugar and orange rind to a very thick cream; gradually beat in the ground almonds. Beat the whites of the eggs perfectly stiff, then add to the rest. Beat all well together. Butter rather shallow cake tins and strew them with very fine brown crumbs. Put in the mixture and bake in a very slow oven for an hour.

Mrs. WORTHINGTON, Duffield.

Yorkshire Parkin

2 lbs. of fine oatmeal	6 oz. of butter
1 lb. of flour	1¾ lbs. of treacle (golden syrup)
¼ lb. of coarse moist sugar (real Demerara if possible)	1 oz. of ginger, powdered

Mix flour, oatmeal, sugar and ginger together, melt the butter and stir it in, warm the treacle and mix to a stiff paste. Roll slightly and cut into round cakes ⅓ inch thick. Bake in a moderate oven 20 minutes.

Mrs. C. W. DIXON, Edgbaston.

Yorkshire Gingerbread

½ lb. of meal, ½ lb. of flour, ¼ lb. of butter or dripping, ½ lb. of syrup, 2 ozs. of sugar, 2 teaspoonfuls of baking powder.

Mrs. PHILIP SNOWDEN, London.

Veronica's Scone

1 lb. of flour	Pinch of salt
New milk or skim	Teaspoonful of sugar
Piece of butter or lard, size of a	Teaspoonful of cream of tartar
walnut	½ teaspoonful of carbonate of soda

Rub the butter into the flour, add sugar, salt and the cream of tartar, dry. Let the carbonate of soda meantime dissolve in a teacupful of hot water, in a basin to which add enough milk to make a not stiff paste. Take a knife and stir in the watery milk by degrees. Flour a board and make into a cake, roll out an inch thick (not less). Put on to a hot girdle (not floured); when sufficiently cooked turn over (put the girdle on the stove without removing the ring). Can be re-heated in oven next day for a few minutes.

Little scones for tea, the same, only cut in long shape or square, but thinner, about ½ inch thick. Mrs. GAYTON, Merstham.

Carraway Seed Biscuits

1 lb. of flour	¼ lb. of butter
¼ lb. of castor sugar	½ oz. of carraway seeds

Work the butter into the flour, mix in the sugar and carraway seeds and moisten to a fairly stiff paste with 1 egg and some ale. Roll out as thin as possible, prick over with a fork and cut into rounds with a cutter. A teaspoonful of baking powder and a little milk or water may be used instead of ale.

Miss WARREN, Hampstead.

Chocolate Macaroons

(*Original*)

1 white of egg	1 teaspoonful of icing sugar
¼ lb. of almonds (peeled and	2 oz. of grated chocolate
chopped fine)	A little vanilla

Stir the sugar and the chocolate into the white of an egg, and then the almonds, flavour to taste with vanilla (it depends on the quality of your chocolate). It should be a stiff paste. Put small blobs on a papered tin and bake in quick oven for 10 minutes.

Mrs. C. W. DIXON, Edgbaston.

Currant Biscuits

6 ozs. of currants

6 ozs. of pounded sugar

½ lb. of butter

¾ lb. of sifted flour

3 yolks of eggs

A little grated nutmeg

Rub butter into flour, add other ingredients, and bind them with 3 beaten yolks of eggs. Roll the mixture out and cut into shapes with tin cutter or tumbler. Bake 10 or 15 minutes, very pale brown.

Mrs. C. W. DIXON, Edgbaston.

Grit Cakes

1 egg, its weight in flour, butter, ground rice and sugar, 1 teaspoonful of baking powder and a very little milk. Beat eggs, white and yolk separately, cream the butter, add other ingredients, white of egg last of all. Bake in buttered patty-pans.

Mrs. C. W. DIXON, Edgbaston.

Rusks

1½ lbs. of flour

½ lb. of butter

2 eggs

3 teaspoonfuls of baking powder

Mix the ingredients and roll out the paste, cut in rounds and bake. Before they are quite done cut them in half with a sharp knife, then put them back into a cool oven for 3 or 4 hours to crisp.

Mrs. G. A. SCHULTZ, Eastbury.

Invalid Cookery

A Good Soup for an Invalid

1 lb. of lean beaf   1 oz. of barley
1 lb. of veal

Boil till tender in 2 quarts of water. Pass through a sieve, salt and pepper but not too much.

Mrs. GERARD DOWSON, Radcliffe-on-Trent.

Brains

(*For Invalids*)

Take a set of brains and boil them in a muslin bag. Have ready some toast. Take out brains when done, chop them fine, spread on the toast, sprinkle with salt, pepper, and a little butter. Put them back in the oven for a few minutes to heat them up.

Mrs. JULIAN OSLER, Edgbaston.

Cake Suitable for Invalids

1 lb. of well-dried flour
½ lb. of butter
¾ lb. of sultanas, washed and well
    dried
½ lb. of sugar

1 teaspoonful of carbonate of soda
3 ozs. of candied lemon-peel, cut
    into small pieces
½ pint of cold milk
2 tablespoonfuls of milk

Mix the flour, sultanas, sugar, and peel together, dry; whip the butter into a cream, and mix it with the other ingredients. Add the ½ pint of cold milk. Beat for 5 minutes. Mix the soda with the 2 tablespoonfuls of milk and add it to the rest of the ingredients. Bake in buttered tins for 2 hours.

Miss G. E. HADOW, Foss Lodge, Cirencester.

Cough Mixture

1 drachm of salts of tartar   10 grains of cochineal (bruised)
½ pint of boiling water

Sweeten with honey, sugar, or sugar-candy (good for whooping cough). DOSE: A dessertspoonful 3 times a day.

Miss DOROTHEA M. GOLDRING, Claygate.

Cure for Jaundice

Peel 3 large lemons, squeeze the juice into a pint of white wine; 2 ozs. of powdered sugar-candy; 2 pennyworth of saffron. Stir all well together, and take a wineglassful every morning.

Miss SHEPPARD, London.

Lemon Solid

(A good dish for a change for invalid not allowed "solid" food.)

1 oz. of gelatine soaked for not less than an hour in cold water, rather more than enough to cover. Add ½ pint of cold water, and stand on hob, or cool side of stove, in saucepan. Peel thinly off the yellow part of rind of 4 (washed) lemons, take away all white pulpy rind, cut rest of lemons into strips, with yellow part of rind, put all this and juice into saucepan with 12 ozs. of sifted sugar, 4 eggs, *not* beaten, ½ pint more of cold water; stir all well together, do not beat, and be sure it does not boil. Leave in this gentle warmth till all gelatine and sugar are dissolved. Strain through a sieve into a mould or basin ready wetted with cold water, and cool till solid and ready to turn out. (This will be an opaque jelly, and containing practically the whole of the eggs is more nourishing than most jellies.) Quantities reduced proportionately to 1 egg make about a ½ pint cup full, just a pleasant dish for invalid.

Miss HELEN E. DOWNS, Brixton.

Linseed Tea

(For a cold)

½ small cup of whole linseed   1½ pints of water
1 lemon rind and juice   Honey to taste

Wash the linseed with cold water, put into saucepan with cold water and bring to boil. Boil for 5 minutes. Pour over lemon and honey. This is excellent for a cough.

Mrs. GAYTON, Merstham.

Medical Plum Jam

(*For indigestion*)

1 lb. of prunes
1 lb. of Demerara sugar
1 oz. of ground ginger

1½ ozs. of powdered senna
1½ glasses of brandy

Put water enough to cover prunes in a pan, simmer very slowly till quite soft, take away the stones and while the prunes are hot add all the other ingredients. Mix well, keep in a jar with a cover over it in winter. This jam will keep for months, but in summer it is apt to ferment. Dose ¼ or ½ or whole teaspoonful as required. Should be taken at bedtime for 6 months; this usually cures constipation in persons under 36, older people require it always. It is a good aperient for children.

Miss MILDRED MARTINEAU, Esher.

Miscellanies

Useful Weights and Measures

Solids

			Measures
¼ lb. of breadcrumbs	-	-	1 breakfast-cupful
¼ lb. of flour	-	-	1 teacupful
1 oz. of sugar, rice, etc.	-	-	1 tablespoonful
1 oz. of butter	-	-	1 tablespoonful
1 oz. dry	-	-	1 small tablespoonful

Liquids

4 saltspoonfuls	-	-	1 teaspoonful
2 teaspoonfuls	-	-	1 dessertspoonful
4 teaspoonfuls	-	-	1 tablespoonful
1 small teacupful	-	-	1 gill
2 small breakfast-cupfuls	-	-	1 pint
4 small breakfast-cupfuls	-	-	1 quart
4 tablespoonfuls	-	-	1 wineglassful
12 tablespoonfuls	-	-	1 teacupful
½ pint	-	-	1 tumblerful
1 pint	-	-	1 pound

Mrs. MORGANS, Claverdon.

A Hint

Instead of chopping onions, a coarse nutmeg grater should be kept for the purpose and the onion should be grated like lemon rind.

Miss IRENE DOWSON, Claygate.

Baby's Blanket

Double Knitting

1 lb. of wool: "AA Peacock Qual. Fleecy" or "Ladyship Super Petticoat Fingering." Needles: size 4. Length: 14 inches.

Cast on 90 stitches.

Knit 16 rows (8 ribs) plain knitting.

17th row: knit 8 stitches plain, knit 2 stitches into each of the next 74, knit the last 8 stitches plain.

18th row and every succeeding row until the blanket is long enough: knit plain the first and last 8 stitches and the intervening ones in double knitting.

Double knitting. Knit 1 and slip 1 alternately, before slipping 1 pass the wool in front of the needle and back again before knitting the next stitch. The first stitch of the double knitting should always be knitted, the last one slipped. In each row you knit the stitches you slipped in the row before.

Finish the blanket with 16 rows of plain knitting.

Miss JULIA SHARPE, Great Missenden.

For Burns

40 grains of picric acid	20 ozs. of distilled water
1 oz. of alcohol	

This mixture to be used in the proportions of 1 of the mixture to 2 of water. Soak lint in it and lay on the burns.

or

Carron oil, which is equal parts of linseed oil and lime water, thoroughly shaken. Paint on the burn and soak bandages in it.

Mrs. SWANWICK, Manchester.

For stewing Apples and Pears

Use brown sugar for stewing pears and white for apples. Dust white sugar over apples directly they are peeled to prevent discoloration. Brown sugar gives a darker, richer colour to pears.

Mrs. GAYTON, Merstham.

For Strained Ankle or Wrist

Brush the part affected with raw white of egg, this will harden and form a crust. Repeat every half hour about 6 times. In the morning the swelling and pain will probably have almost disappeared.

Miss MABEL THOMAS, Bristol.

Four Useful Hints for Everyday Cookery

I.

Are you troubled by custard puddings that are watery and curdled?

Place the dish containing the pudding in another and a larger dish filled with water. This will enable you to bake a good custard pudding even in a very hot oven.

Mrs. ROBIE UNIACKE, Andover.

II.

Is the breakfast bacon hard and tough?

To rectify this be sure the bacon is cut very thin; only a sharp bacon knife will do this satisfactorily. Heat the frying-pan through before you put the bacon on it; this can be done by holding the pan over the fire until it begins to smoke slightly. If these two rules are observed 3 to 5 minutes should cook the bacon, which must be served quickly and eaten at once.

Mrs. ROBIE UNIACKE, Andover.

III.

If you want to fry fish successfully let the fat you fry it in be boiling before the fish is put into it. This applies particularly to plaice, which is a watery fish.

Mrs. ROBIE UNIACKE, Andover.

IV.

To make a really delicious dish of "stewed raspberries" don't stew them! Make a rich syrup with red currants and sugar and place the raspberries in it uncooked. If red currants are not available the syrup may be made with raspberries and sugar.

Mrs. ROBIE UNIACKE, Andover.

Furniture Polish

I.

½ pint of linseed oil
¼ pint of methylated spirit
2 ozs. of spirits of turpentine

2 ozs. of brown vinegar
½ oz. of butyr antimony

Mix well and shake before using.

Miss SHEPPARD, London.

E

Furniture Polish

II.

½ oz. of good yellow soap
3 ozs. of beeswax
1 pint of turpentine

1 oz. of white wax
1 pint of water

Shred the beeswax and white wax into the turpentine and melt on the side of the stove. Care must be taken that it does not boil over as it would easily catch fire. Dissolve the soap in the pint of water (hot), stir both mixtures together while warm and put into jars or bottles.

Miss WARREN, Hampstead.

To make Good Bread

(*American*)

Dough should be mixed *as soft as it can be handled.* The bread rises sooner and higher, is lighter and more digestible and keeps fresh longer.

Mrs. ALFRED BOOTH, Liverpool.

To freshen Stale Cake or Bread

To freshen stale cake or bread dip it for a second in cold milk and bake it in a rather cold oven.

Mrs. BRACKENBURY, Gomshall.

For Roasting Beef

When roasting beef in the oven dash a small cup of *boiling* water over the meat in first putting it down, letting it trickle into the pan. This, for a time, checks the escape of the juices and allows the meat to get warmed through before the top dries by said escape.

Mrs. ATKINSON, Camberley.

Hints

I.

Rub ivory knife handles with turpentine to restore their colour when they have turned yellow.

II.

If food becomes slightly burnt while cooking, set the pan at once in a basin of cold water and its flavour will be uninjured.

III.

Brooms will last longer if dipped occasionally into boiling suds.

Miss ALICE JACKSON, Nottingham.

For Sponge Cakes

Rub the mould with best Lucca oil and dust thickly over with finest flour and finest castor sugar mixed in the proportion of 2 of flour to 1 of sugar. This gives a sponge cake appearance to the outside. If greased with butter they are more likely to stick on account of the salt in the butter.

Mrs. GAYTON, Merstham.

How to Set Colours

Saltpetre or alum can be used for blues or greens, 1 oz. to 12 quarts of boiling water. 1 oz. of sugar of lead dissolved in 12 quarts of boiling water is good for any colour except blue. 1 tablespoonful of soda to 12 quarts of boiling water will set pink or blue. 1 tablespoonful of black pepper to 12 quarts of boiling water will set any of the greys, buffs or tans.

Miss SHEPPARD, London.

Method of washing Handkerchiefs when travelling

Wash handkerchiefs out in the usual way, squeeze out the water well and spread out on a window-pane, where they will stick readily. Smooth out the creases and leave to dry. If done over night they will peel off nicely by the morning and look as if they had been ironed.

Mrs. VINCENT, Camberley.

Moths in Carpets

Moths in the carpet may be got rid of by scrubbing the floor with strong, hot, salt water, before the carpet is put down, and then sprinkling the carpet with salt when it is being swept.

Miss SHEPPARD, London.

To Bore Holes in Leather Straps

Heat a hair-pin in a candle, or a skewer in the kitchen fire, and apply to both sides of the strap at the desired point.

Miss E. M. GARDNER, Birmingham.

To clean Indian Brass

(Not for polished surface)

Take 1 tablespoonful of flour
2 tablespoonfuls of silver sand

3 tablespoonfuls of vinegar (best malt)
A pinch of salt

Make into a paste, rub in with a brush, wash off with cold water, dry with soft cloth. Put in front of the fire or sun and when warm rub well with a dry cloth.

Mrs. VINCENT, Camberley.

To clean Mackintosh

Lay it flat on a table and rub it over with a nail-brush dipped in soft water and yellow soap. After the dirt is removed rinse the garment several times in clean cold water. Do not wring it, but shake it well, then hang it in the open air to dry.

Miss SHEPPARD, London.

To clean Natural Wood Kitchen Tables

Cut a lemon in two and rub it over the surface, rinsing it well with clean warm water; the result will be a snowy white board without the rough top made by continual scrubbing with a brush.

Miss SHEPPARD, London.

To clean Paint

Squeeze a clean cloth out of hot water, dip it in whitening and with this rub the paint until quite clean. Rinse it well with clean water, dry it with a soft cloth, and polish it with a chamois leather. This will render paint as good as new and will not harm even delicate colours.

Miss SHEPPARD, London.

To clean Straw Matting

Wash with a cloth dipped in clean salt and water, then wipe dry at once. This prevents it from turning yellow.

Miss BOOTH, Liverpool.

To cook French Beans which have been preserved in pans in layers of salt

Put them into a pan and let them soak for an hour in water, take out and rinse all the salt off; put them into a saucepan with enough water to boil them, and a little soda to keep the colour, but *no* salt. Partly boil them, say a quarter of an hour; then strain off all that water thoroughly and boil again in fresh water for another quarter of an hour.

Mrs. ATKINSON, Camberley.

To exterminate Ants

Wring out a sponge in a solution of sugar and water and put on a plate in the room infested with the insects. Very soon it will be filled with ants and may be plunged into boiling water to get rid of them, and may be used again in the same way.

Miss SHEPPARD, London.

To get Stains off Brown Boots

Dissolve a little salts of lemon in water, then rub the stain with a clean rag that has been dipped in the mixture, constantly using a fresh bit of rag. Then polish.

Miss WALFORD, Kingswood.

To improve colour of Tan Boots

Take one pennyworth of liquid ammonia and mix it with 1 gill of milk, then shake the bottle and apply the mixture with a sponge, leave it to dry, and then polish with a soft brush.

Miss SHEPPARD, London.

To make Basins and Pans Fireproof

(*Excellent*)

Have a large boiler (an old-fashioned copper is best). Place in it the pan or basin you wish to make fireproof, just new. Put in cold water and bring slowly to the boil, let it boil a few minutes, take it off and let the pans stay in the water till quite cold, they will then not crack when used for hot liquids or in the oven. Have a piece of wood at the bottom of the boiler so that the pan or basins stand on it during the process.

Mrs. GAYTON, Merstham.

To preserve Flowers

Cut the stems in a long slanting cut, and place them in fresh water, do not let the stems touch the bottom of vase. Before putting in the flowers put a little powdered charcoal in the water.

Miss SHEPPARD, London.

To remove Scratches on Furniture

Place a coarse cloth well saturated with linseed oil on the damaged portion and allow it to remain on with a little pressure for some time. Then remove it and rub the furniture over lightly with a soft duster.

Miss SHEPPARD, London.

To smooth wrinkled Silk

Sponge on the right side with very weak gum arabic water and iron on the wrong side.

Miss BOOTH, Liverpool.

To take out Iron-mould

1 oz. of salts of sorrel (powdered), mixed with 2 ozs. of cream of tartar. Apply to spots and rinse well in cold water.

Miss SHEPPARD, London.

To wash Coloured Silks

Use bran water and the colour will not run. Put 3 or 4 handfuls of bran into a piece of muslin and pour boiling water over it and when it is cool enough wash the silk with it, not using any soap. Dry it quickly and then iron it on the wrong side.

Miss SHEPPARD, London.

To wash Woollen Garments

To wash knitted garments so that they will not shrink, make some warm soapsuds, using water just as hot as the hands can bear it and pure soap only. Do not rub the soap on the garments but let the suds and wringer do the work. Put the garments through the wringer and back into the suds two or three times, rub them very little and do not use a washing board. Rinse the garments thoroughly in clear water, then stretch them lengthways and dry quickly in the open air.

Miss Sheppard, London.

Use for Boxes

Keep the wax-coated boxes in which crackers are packed, for they make excellent polishers for irons, instead of the little blocks of paraffin wax generally used.

Miss Sheppard, London.

MENUS FOR MEALS FOR SUFFRAGE WORKERS

It is not always easy to provide suitable food for workers who have to get their meals as best they can during a day's hard and exacting work often lasting for 12 hours or more. It is essential that the meals should be sustaining and yet they must be simple and such as can be eaten quickly, and also made up of dishes which will keep hot without spoiling and can be eaten with impunity at any hour.

The following suggestions are an attempt to cope with the difficulty:

Luncheon

I.

Mutton Cutlets
Cold Beef and Potato Salad

—

Victoria Sandwich
Chocolate Jelly

II.

Poached Eggs on Spinach
Fillets of Beef or Haricot Mutton

—

Cold Custard Pudding
Stewed Fruit

III.

Cold Chicken and Ham
Sweetbreads in White Sauce

Cold Caramel Pudding
Arrowroot Pudding

Supper

I.

Egg Flip

—

Chicken in casserole

—

Apple and Sago Pudding
Junket

II.

Chicken Broth

—

Fish Pudding

—

Cold Leg of Lamb and Salad

—

Bread and Butter Pudding
Apple Snow

III.

Gravy Soup

—

Chicken Rissoles or Chicken Cream

—

Galantine of Turkey and Tongue

—

Milk Jelly
Summer Pudding (Bread and Fruit
with Custard)

RECIPE FOR COOKING AND PRESERVING A GOOD SUFFRAGE SPEAKER

First: Butter the speaker, when asking her to come, with a stamped and addressed envelope, post-card, or telegraph form for reply.

Second: Grease the dish by paying all the speaker's expenses.

Third: Put her to cool or to warm, as the case may be, in a room by herself before the meeting, so that she may be fresh and in good condition for speaking.

Fourth: Beat her to a froth with an optimistic spoon, making light of all disappointments. Carefully avoid too strong a flavour of apologies.

Fifth: Do not let her cool too rapidly after the meeting, but place her considerately by a nice bedroom fire, with a light supper to be taken in solitude.

(If this recipe is carefully followed, the speaker will be found to preserve her flavour to the last moment, and will do her utmost to make the meeting a success.)

Mrs. BERTRAND RUSSELL, Bagley Wood.

Index

Glossary

bloater paste Fish spread made from salted, smoked herrings called 'bloaters'.

carmine Cochineal extract.

chafing dish A kind of portable grate raised on a tripod. Used for foods that require gentle cooking away from direct flames.

coralline pepper Most likely paprika.

drachm Also called fluid dram. Equivalent to ⅛ fl oz.

filtering paper A porous paper used for filtering liquids.

gill A unit of measurement no longer in common usage, except for volume of alcoholic spirit measures. Equivalent to 5 fl oz.

Glacialine A milk preservative.

hair sieve A strainer with a haircloth bottom. Substitute with a sieve with a fine mesh.

isinglass Gelatine made from the air bladders of freshwater fish.

kiver A shallow vessel or wooden tub.

loaf sugar Also pounded sugar. Refined sugar moulded into loaves or cubes. This was the usual form in which refined sugar was produced and sold until the late nineteenth century. People would shave off the sugar they needed from the block or pound it to a specific amount for a recipe. Substitute with granulated sugar.

Lucca oil Olive oil from the region of Lucca.

Plasmon stock Possibly a type of baby milk powder.

powdered sugar Also known as confectioner's sugar. Use icing sugar.

protose A meal substitute made chiefly from wheat gluten and peanuts, popular in the early twentieth century.

salamander Traditionally a heated metal disc used to brown or finish a dish. Today it describes a self-contained broiler unit.

salts of tartar Potassium carbonate.

sippet A small piece of bread or toast, used to dip into soups or sauces, or as a garnish.
stone milled flour Stoneground flour.
waterglass Silicate of soda.
white paper Substitute with greaseproof paper.

Specific oven temperatures are not given in the recipes. Use the following guide:

very slow/cool 110-135°C (225-275°F), Gas mark ¼-1
slow/low oven: 150°C (300°F), Gas mark 2
warm oven: 165°C (325°F), Gas mark 3
moderate/medium oven: 175°C (350°F), Gas mark 4
quick oven: 205°C (400°F), Gas mark 6
hot oven: 220°C (425°F), Gas mark 7
very hot: 230-245°C (450-475°F), Gas mark 8-9

First published in 1912 by the Women's Printing Society Limited

This edition first published in 2020 by
The British Library
96 Euston Road
London NW1 2DB

Foreword copyright © 2020 Polly Russell
Design copyright © 2020 The British Library Board

Cataloguing in Publication Data
A catalogue record for this publication is available from The British Library

ISBN 978 0 7123 5375 5
Printed and bound by Finidr, Czech Republic